RHYTHMIC MEDICINE

RHYTHMIC MEDICINE

MUSIC WITH A PURPOSE

JANALEA HOFFMAN

JAMILLAN PRESS

ISBN 1-886051-18-6

First printing 1995.

Printed in the U.S.A.

Jamillan Press
P.O. Box 6431
Leawood, KS 66206

Also by Janalea Hoffman

Music Cassettes

Children's Meditation Tape

Crisis Tape

Deep Daydreams

Mind Body Tempo

Music for Mellow Minds

Music, Imagery, and Parkinson's

Music to Facilitate Imagery

Musical Acupuncture

Musical Biofeedback

Musical Hypnosis

Musical Massage

Therapeutic Drumming

Touched By the Light

CD's

Deep Daydreams

Musical Acupuncture

Musical Massage

Video's

Rhythmic Medicine

Instructional Video

MUSIC WITH A PURPOSE CASSETTE TAPE

An all music cassette specifically designed to use
with the exercises in this book

A message from the author, Janalea Hoffman:

Being a musician and music therapist, I know the importance of *experiencing* the therapeutic techniques using music that I have illustrated in this book. It is difficult to find the specific music I refer to in the musical biofeedback exercises and the inner child exercises, so, for your convenience, I have produced a 60 minute, all music cassette tape that works in coordination with the exercises.

The tape includes:

▶ Side 1: 30 minutes of music at exactly 50 beats per minute for use with exercises at the end of chapter 2. All acoustic (natural) instruments.

▶ Side 2: Seven different selections of music that correspond to the following inner child exercises at the end of chapter 4. 30 minutes, 85% natural instruments.
    1. Remembering Gifts
    2. The Angry Inner Child
    3. The Sad Inner Child
    4. The Playful Inner Child
    5. The Powerful Inner Child
    6. The Joyful Inner Child
    7. The Wise Inner Child

Please send me _____ copy(s) of the *Music With a Purpose* **cassette tape at $9.95 each.** *

Send to:

Name: _____

Address: _____   _____

City: _____   State: _____   Zip: _____

Phone: _____   Check enclosed: _____

MC/Visa #: _____ Exp: _____

* Shipping and handling, $2.50 per order.

PREFACE

When I say I am a music therapist, many people form the mental image of someone walking down an aisle of a psychiatric hospital with a guitar slung over their back and rhythm band instruments hanging on their body, clanging and banging as they walk down the corridor. This is one aspect of music therapy. However, there are many styles and methods of using music as a healing tool. This book is about some of the methods I have developed over the years in a private practice.

I have found that most people intuitively believe in the healing power of music; however, they have no idea how to specifically unlock this power. Even the ancients believed in the healing power of music. In the Old Testament there is the story of Saul, an old king who was suffering and given the following advice (1 Samuel 16:16):

> *"Seek out a man, who is a wise player on a harp and it shall come to pass . . . that he shall play with his hand and thou shall be well."*

The king sent for David with the following results (I Samuel 16:23):

> *"David took a harp, and played with his hand and Saul was refreshed, and was well, and the evil spirit departed from him."*

It is obvious from this and other stories that the ancients understood the healing power of music and used it in their lives. Usually, there is mention of playing the music. But specific techniques are never mentioned, and if they are, they are often so esoteric that most of us in the 20th century, cannot relate. It is obvious that playing music is not enough. Because if it were true, you could go to a concert and be healed! It is quite possible to go to a concert and be moved emotionally or gain a new insight by quietly listening to the music, but if everyone was healed, aspirin and other drug sales would plummet!

Part of my personal and professional quest has been to explore this healing concept and to develop specific techniques with music that can achieve measurable results. There is a lot of suffering in our world, and more and more people are seeking natural cures. It is important that the arts be explored as an avenue for self-expression and natural healing.

In my quest to extract the power of music, I have found rhythm to be one of the most powerful tools that can be measured as having a therapeutic benefit. This is explored in the first three chapters of this book. The fact that rhythm is also found in other art forms makes it a more universal element than harmony and melody, the other two important elements of music. For example, you find rhythmic lines in art forms such as painting and sculpture. The fact that rhythm is so interwoven in all art forms brings up the argument that it could be considered more important than the other two elements and possibly even placed in the cosmic category. This idea is supported in Chapter One, Music and the Heart – The Power of Rhythm. It is difficult to separate the melody from the harmony and determine which one is the most beneficial. It is easier to separate the rhythm and research this aspect.

This book was written for therapists, musicians, non-musicians and anyone seeking natural healing or deeper understanding of the psyche. These exercises can be used in your own home for your own personal empowerment. Many people will try them as an adjunct to their ongoing therapy. In this connection, a friend asked the question, "What if someone gets in touch with a traumatic experience with the inner child exercises that they can not handle on their own?" My experience has been that when you are using natural healing methods like these, the psyche door does not open so quickly that it becomes a problem, as opposed to drugs, which open the psyche door too quickly and, therefore, can create trauma. If you find that old memories emerge from the music that are troubling, remember, it is much better to feel deeply than to be numb inside. As you work through the exercises, you may find it helpful to further explore the issues that arise through journaling, artwork, clay, movement therapy, walking, etc.

As far as I know, this is the first self-help music therapy book written for a main-stream audience. Reading about music without hearing it, is similar to reading food reviews in the newspaper and not tasting the food. Needless to say, it is better to hear the music and taste the food. That is why a tape is available with this book if the reader desires to hear the therapeutic music and follow through with the exercises. The tape includes the fifty beats-a-minute-music and also the music for the inner child exercises. Other therapeutic music mentioned in the book is listed in the Sources of Sound section.

I hope you will enjoy reading this book and exploring some or all of the exercises. Music has an ethereal quality to it that can uplift, bring joy and even heal physical conditions. Exploring feelings is so much more fun and rewarding with the aid of music. Music can lead you on a very exciting inner journey.

INTRODUCTION

Music has been very significant to me all my life. As a child, I studied piano from the age of six, entered into music contests from the age of seven, and have been playing music ever since. When I was a child, music provided a means of emotional release and self-expression that was not available to me in any other way. Now we know that children who study music for at least three years do better scholastically and emotionally than children who do not study music. When it was time for me to go to college, I never thought about a major. Rather I just *knew* that I would study music. As I was working on my senior recital at the conservatory for organ performance, it dawned on me that I was spending four hours a day practicing in a big, lonely church, yet, I considered myself to be an extrovert. I had spent two years learning a Bach Toccata with a pedal solo. After feeling a few moments of pride about that, it dawned on me that I didn't want to be a church organist, a professional musician, or a performer. My inner light bulb went off and I realized that my real interests were in the effects of music on humanity. As a result, how music affects us emotionally and physically became my passion for exploration! A few months after I finished my degree in organ performance, I went back to school and completed a degree in music therapy to achieve this goal.

After working in a state psychiatric hospital for 14 months right after receiving my degree in music therapy, I decided to start my own business and specialize in a synthesis of music, relaxation and imagery work. My studies with Helen Bonny and The Institute for Consciousness and Music inspired me to find out all I could about guided imagery with music - GIM. The idea of music, altered states of consciousness and delving into the unconscious was very exciting to me. My enthusiasm for understanding the foundations for these ideas led me back to college where I earned a masters in music therapy.

The techniques in this book were all born out of my private practice – years of working with people on a daily basis using music and relaxation techniques. My client base consists mainly of professional, creative, productive people, all seeking a natural cure for some stress-related problem. They are all open-minded, but demand that the techniques have to be practical and work. Thus they are not patient with very esoteric ideas, "like the key of D will heal your liver." Working with these people has been a gift because it has forced me to come up with creative solutions. Hence I developed the techniques found in this book.

I have found that music is a key factor in helping people go deep enough that they really *feel* something dramatic happen. We live in an "add water and stir" society. Everyone wants something very fast, including their relaxation experiences. Nobody wants to sit quietly for months waiting for the *one* big experience. Music helps take people into very deep states of consciousness that are usually rewarding enough so that they are motivated to continue working with it.

I have found that the rhythmic aspects of music are a powerful tool in slowing down the body so that the mind can also slow down long enough to find new insights. In my frustration at not readily being able to find very slow rhythms to use with clients, I began to write music myself at 60 beats a minute and later at 50 beats a minute. Much of the classical literature is very beautiful and can be used therapeutically; however, there is not much available to facilitate deep meditative work. Also, since most of the music that I was writing didn't fit into any contemporary categories, I developed the concept of *therapeutic music.* I am confident that the future will bring many new applications of my music. There is a need to create specific music for specific problems. For example, my tape, *Musical Hypnosis*, has music that starts at 80 beats a minute and slowly moves to 50-beats-a-minute music. The idea is that your body tries to synchronize, so you use this music to lower heart rate and blood pressure.

One of the surprises in my work using music occurred when people had spontaneous spiritual experiences. There is a cosmic aspect to music that cannot be explained. A friend of mine in England said, "Of all the arts, music is the most spiritual." His basis for that statement was that you can't touch it or destroy it. Once it is created, it is vibration and has an ethereal effect. It is very rewarding to be helping someone lower their blood pressure with music and, as a side benefit, have them experience something deeper on a spiritual level and watch them walk away with a magical smile on their face.

Socrates and Jesus both said, "Know thyself." The musical biofeedback exercises with music in this book are all about knowing your body better. Einstein said that everything you need to know you can learn from observing your body. This is a concept that can be hard to grasp because it gets into the mystical realm. The techniques in this book can help you to understand this concept. The exercises with music range from lowering heart rate, to contacting your inner child, to increasing inner power. There are also exercises about using songs as affirmations, as well as a *Diagnostic Music Self-Test* that helps you ana-lyze your overall music listening habits. That is, what your musical pref-erences, patterns, and resistances symbolize about your emotional issues.

The real musical genius writes for no other purpose but to express his own Soul, and in so doing, finds life's greatest satisfaction and joy. This quote by the great composer Delius is one of the reasons why there is such healing power in music. It is the soulful quality of a great piece of music that draws out our own soul-felt feelings that are often buried deeply under layers of conditioning and social pressure. The exercises in this book are designed to help you explore the many layers of consciousness. I believe that we all have a purpose for being here and that we possess talents, which, when channelled properly, bring us and others tremendous joy. I hope you will enjoy your inner journey as you read this book and experience the exercises.

ACKNOWLEDGMENTS

My thanks go to my parents for encouraging me to express myself through music at an early age. Their support in music was always loving and consistent.

Much gratitude goes to Marilyn Miller who offered consistent moral support and encouragement. She ran the company called Rhythmic Medicine while I wrote the book. Without her support, this book would have taken another ten years to write!

Also thanks goes to Kirsten McBride, Kim Tappan, Carol Prietschmann and Bette Harrod for their advice and encouragement.

CONTENTS

Preface i

Introduction iii

Acknowledgements vi

Chapter 1: Music and Your Heart – The Power of Rhythm 1
    The Relationship Between Body Rhythms 1
        and Musical Rhythms
    Entrainment 3
        How Entrainment Can Effect You Negatively 5
        General Examples of Entrainment 8
        How Entrainment Can Improve Your Life. 10
        Entrainment and Improved Learning Abilities 13

Chapter 2: Entrainment and Musical
        Biofeedback – How They Relate 18
    Mental Activity and Its Physiological Effects 22
    Motivation for Learning the Musical Biofeedback Process 24
    Reasons for Combining Imagery and Music 25
    Increased Sensitivity 26
    Why It Is Important to Be Able to Feel Your Heart Beat 27
    Musical Biofeedback Exercises 27
        Musical Biofeedback Exercise for Heart Beat 29
            Processing the Heart Beat Exercise 31
        Musical Biofeedback for Breathing Rate Exercise 34
            Processing the Breathing Rate Exercise 35
        Musical Biofeedback for Blood Pressure Control Exercise . . . 37
            Processing the Blood Pressure Exercise 38
            Evaluation of Blood Pressure Exercise. 39

Chapter 3: Music and Lowering Blood Pressure 42
    Body Awareness and Hypertension. 45
        What Is Hypertension / High Blood Pressure? 46
        Reasons Why People Fail to Follow 52
            Through with Medication

Chapter 4: Using Music to Help Contact the Inner Child 55
   Why It Can Be Difficult to Communicate with the Inner Child . . . 58
   Why Does Inner Child Music Work So Well in 59
     Communicating with Our Inner Child?
   Examples of Different Aspects of the Inner Child 61
     The Angry Child and Its Relationship to Illness 61
     Sad Inner Child and Depression 65
     Powerful Inner Child 66
   Exercises to Process the Inner Child. 70
     Remembering Gifts 72
     The Angry Inner Child 75
     The Sad Inner Child. 78
     The Playful Inner Child 81
     The Powerful Inner Child 84
     The Joyful Inner Child 87
     The Wise Inner Child 89

Chapter 5: Music and Codependency 92
   What Is Codependency? 92
   How Codependency Relates to Music. 96
   Addiction to Chaotic Sound 99
   Core Symptoms of Codependency 100
     Giving Your Power Away 101
       Exercise: Giving Your Power Away 103
     Poor Boundaries 104
       Exercise: Poor Boundaries 105
     Denial 106
     Looking for Love Outside Ourselves 108
     Codependency and/or Caretaking 109
   Music Diagnostic Self-Test. 116
     Evaluation of Music Diagnostic Self-Test 123

Chapter 6: Positive Songs – Songs for Recovery 126
   Song Lyrics and Positive Affirmation – Are They Related? 129
   Why Use Musical Affirmations Over Spoken Affirmations? 131
   Songs About Overcoming 132
   Why Is It Important to Sing the Songs? 136
   Songs for Recovery. 137
   Songs About Grief and Loss 141
   Songs That Match Your Mood 144

Exercise: Match a Feeling to a Song 147
Positive Song Exercise 148

Chapter 7: Inner Power Through Music 151
Quiet Inner Power. 154
Spiritual Power 155
Energized Power. 156
Physical Power 157
Power from Risk Taking. 158
Power from Love. 160
Power over Food. 161
Exercises to Process Inner Power 164
Quiet Inner Power 164
Spiritual Power 166
Energized Power 168
Physical Power 170
Power Through Risk Taking 172
Power from Love 174
Power over Food 176
Comments on My Musical Choices for Inner Power Exercises . . . 178

References. 182

Sources of Sound 186

CHAPTER 1

MUSIC AND YOUR HEART – THE POWER OF RHYTHM

From the moment of conception, when our cells began to divide and multiply in a womb that quivers to our mother's pulse, to the last fibrillation of our own dying heart, humans are deeply rhythmical creatures, inextricably woven into an intricate web of pattern and pulsation. We're a bundle of oscillating brain waves and palpitating cells, stitched together by the ins and outs of our breath. We're perpetually dancing to circadian rhythms of sleeping and waking; metabolic rhythms of eating and elimination; hormonal rhythms of ovulation, puberty, menarche, and menopause. These personal beats, in turn, are inextricably linked with planetary cycles of day and night, the waxing and waning of the moon, and the changing of the seasons.[1]

The Relationship Between Body Rhythms and Musical Rhythms

Everyone responds to sound and rhythm. This is not surprising because, in fact, we are exposed to these stimuli even before we are born. In our mother's womb, the first sound we hear is the sound of her heart beating. This early experience creates an intimate connection between musical rhythms and body rhythms. Once born, we are rocked as babies when we need to be comforted, thereby creating a strong association between relaxation and rhythm. This rocking usually occurs between mother and child – heart to heart – echoing the prenatal experience of the mother's heart rhythm and therefore, further bonding mother and child. From rocking horses as young children we move on to rocking chairs as senior citizens, illustrating that rhythm for soothing purposes does not have anything to do with chronological age.

This relationship between musical rhythms and internal body rhythms is extremely significant. Internal body rhythms play an important role in how relaxed or tense one feels. It is well known, for example, that when people are very tense, their body rhythms undergo many unconscious or unperceived changes. One of the quickest changes to occur in body rhythms is an increased heart rate. This phenomenon is illustrated in the following study.

In a study showing the importance of a slow external rhythm in the relaxation process, volunteers were subjected to a situation that made them extremely anxious and tense. As a result, they experienced an expected increase in heart rate.[2] To illustrate these changes, the research subjects' heartbeats were amplified electronically so they could hear them. The sound they heard was similar to what one would hear in a stethoscope; however, when the heart rates increased due to anxiety, the amplified rapid heartbeats were no longer heard. Instead, a mechanical device made sounds that simulated slow, relaxed heartbeats. When the subjects heard the slow heartbeats, their tension levels decreased and their own heart rates slowed down accordingly.

This example demonstrates the power of rhythm over our heart beats. The false slow heart beats led to relaxation due to the impact of exter-

> *Once born, we are rocked as babies when we need to be comforted, thereby creating a strong association between relaxation and rhythm.*

nal rhythms (mechanical sounds, in this case) on internal rhythms. In other words, the volunteers in this study seemed to accept the relaxed, simulated rhythms as a message that their body was no longer disturbed. Therefore, since their bodies no longer needed to prepare for defense, their anxiety levels decreased.

These results inspired me to start using music at very slow, steady rhythms in deep relaxation training. Often, such slow rhythms de-accelerated body rhythms very dramatically. For example, I use this principle when I play 50-beats-a-minute music. The listener's heart responds to the external stimulus of the slow, steady beat of the music and her/his heart rate begins to synchronize. This phenomenon is called *entrainment*. It is a term that is not widely used, yet entrainment affects everyone, every day. Entrainment, in combination with the right music and techniques, can be excellent preventive medicine

Entrainment

A pediatrician in the neonatal unit of a major training hospital confirmed that he often witnesses the effects of entrainment in his work. For example, nurses in the neonatal unit have observed that babies with normal heart rates placed next to a baby with an irregular heart rate entrain to the irregular beat. When this happens, the staff move the babies' cribs far enough apart so the babies can no longer influence each other negatively. The pediatrician also mentioned that some babies will entrain to the computer monitor sound systems near them.

Entrainment occurs between all living beings with music and with *anything* that creates rhythm. A scientific explanation for entrainment is that any two living vibratory bodies will try to synchronize with each other. This phenomenon was first discovered by a Dutch scientist, who noticed that the pendulums of grandfather clocks tend to swing in synchrony when placed in close proximity to each other.

A metronome set at 60 beats a minute slows down body rhythms because the body tries to harmonize, or entrain, with the external rhythm.[3] Sixty beats a minute is an average relaxed heartbeat. Another example of entrainment is that women living together in dormitories, for example, tend to have their menstrual cycles synchronize.

A common musical example of entrainment may have happened to you. Have you ever walked through a section of a department store that is playing fast-paced rock music and noticed your heart rate, blood pressure and brain waves are all speeding up to try and synchronize with the beat. Although this all happens unconsciously, you may be consciously annoyed, thinking to yourself that you don't like this kind of music. However, it is, in fact, your body that doesn't like the music or the adaptation it is forced to make to stay in harmony. To entrain to the fast music, your body must speed up, which may not be in tune with your relaxed mood as you browse for a new outfit.

To achieve the opposite effect of the fast music in the example above, I use 50- or 60-beats-a-minute music in my therapy sessions. The body's internal rhythms slow down to synchronize with the slower external musical rhythm, making it a very useful tool in body awareness training. Exactly 50 or 60 beats a minute are useful because they correspond to a relaxed heart beat. This specially metered music is extremely effective in helping slow down body rhythms because it gives an individual a point of reference to entrain with. When you are not aware of your inner rhythms, you can't change them, either faster or slower, until you have observed them or have established some point of reference. This is

A metronome set at 60 beats a minute slows down body rhythms because the body tries to harmonize, or entrain, with the external rhythm.

what the specially metered music does. Patients have said, "Until I had this point of reference with rhythm, I was very confused and felt hopeless about controlling my body rhythms. Now it seems very attainable and almost easy."

How Entrainment Can Effect You Negatively

A woman, Gloria, explained during the question-and-answer period after one of my lectures on music and rhythm that she had suffered a heart attack and felt it was because her heart was entraining to the vibration or rhythm in the ice cream shop where she worked. She described the environment as a small shop with five ice cream machines that would come on and off at different times. Imagine the guttural machine-like vibration that refrigerators make. It is not a natural sound and, therefore, tends to be extremely irritating.

Gloria's intuition was very strong that the machine vibrations contributed to her heart problem. It made sense to me that due to the theory of entrainment the refrigerators' erratic rhythm could have had a detrimental effect on her body rhythms. Gloria was distressed that her doctor told her that the ice cream machines had nothing to do with her heart problem. However, her faith in her own intuition was renewed the night she learned of entrainment!

When analyzing this situation in more depth, it is interesting to note that ice cream shops are usually staffed by teenagers whose hormones are already in a state of flux. As a result, they are more able to stand the vibrations of five refrigerators than an older person who requires a more peaceful setting.

My experience with people with heart arrhythmias is that when they practice with the 60- and/or 50-beats-a-minute music on the tapes I

The 50-beats-a-minute music is the only thing Roger has found to relax him as effectively as going to a remote place in the country and lying peacefully in a hammock strung between two oak trees!

have developed and composed, *Deep Daydreams,*[4] *Musical Hypnosis,*[5] or *Therapeutic Drumming,*[6] they can learn to slow their own heart rates and condition their hearts to stay steady even in a stressful state. Apart from cases where heart arrhythmias are completely a physical problem, stress is a major contributor to the problem. Therefore, using a technique I call *musical biofeedback*, in which you match your heart beat and breathing rate to the slow, steady beat of the music (see exercises at end of Chapter 2), you can empower yourself and take control rather than taking drugs or walking around being fearful that you might have a heart attack at any moment.

A client, Marcie, initially came to me because she was suffering from heart palpitations and general anxiety. After three sessions where she learned to match her heart rate to the beat of the music, Marcie was feeling more in control and was managing her stress level very well. Despite this improvement, though, she still suffered heart arrhythmias.

After learning about the power of entrainment over body rhythms, Marcie recalled that she was in the habit of running a fan at night and, therefore, began wondering if the erratic vibration of this old, loud appliance could be affecting her during the night while she slept. To test her hypothesis, she eliminated the fan noise for two weeks, only to discover that her heart palpitation problem improved dramatically.

Roger, an environmentalist, botanist and tree doctor by profession, has a real passion for trees. He loves to talk about them, trim them and do whatever else is necessary to improve their health. Since Roger often trims trees, he uses a chain saw frequently. The loud noise coupled with the adrenaline he needs to stay alert while using this potentially dangerous machine makes him so hyperactive by the end of the day that he has trouble relaxing. In other words, he finds himself entraining to the loud, fast rhythm of the chain saw.

The 50-beats-a-minute music is the only thing Roger has found to relax him as effectively as going to a remote place in the country and lying peacefully in a hammock strung between two oak trees!

The twentieth century brought the advent of machinery, which people in other times did not have to worry about. Before machines, people had more natural phenomena to entrain to. Now the balance between machines, such as the refrigerators in Gloria's ice cream shop, Marcie's fan, and Roger's chain saw, and natural living is a very tight rope to walk.

Many people ask, "If I mask an annoying rhythm with some other sound, such as a wave machine or music that is louder than the sound that needs to be eliminated, will this solve the problem?" Masking the sound or vibration can be helpful, but it does not eliminate the problem. Sound is vibration and even if you cannot physically hear it, the vibration is still affecting your body. For example, an annoying vibration sound, a window air conditioner, still affects your body if you play loud music to mask the vibration.

Since our bodies are *always* trying to synchronize with external rhythms, simply covering an annoying sound with another sound does not eliminate the phenomenon of entrainment. That would be analogous to sweeping dirt under the rug or cleaning the top floor of your house and putting the garbage in the basement. Eventually, the smell and dirt will seep up and effect you in some way.

Marvin, a workshop participant, told me a story that related his farming career to entrainment. When he first began to farm, he drove John Deer, two-cylinder tractors. Later, when he switched to four- and finally six-cylinder tractors, he noticed that he felt much more relaxed and even refreshed after working for hours on the two-cylinder tractors rather than more modern models, which resulted in a more stressed feeling. Consistent with the notion of entrainment, Marvin's explanation was that the two-cylinder machine emitted a much slower rhythm, thus creating a more meditative state as he drove along in the fields.

Consistent with the notion of entrainment, Marvin's explanation was that the two-cylinder machine emitted a much slower rhythm, thus creating a more meditative state as he drove along in the fields.

Priscilla related her experiences that occurred on a 1,500-mile car trip with a friend, who had a habit of biting her fingernails. At the beginning of the trip, Pam didn't think much about this behavior; however, half way into the trip she found herself biting her fingernails. In the close space of the car for many hours, she had begun to entrain with the friend's habit of fingernail biting. This entrainment became so annoying to her that she finally asked her driving companion if she could refrain from biting her fingernails so much.

In addition to more external behaviors, such as those described above, entrainment can occur between a joyful person and a depressed person. That is, the depressed person can pull the joyful person down to his or her level or vice versa. This does not mean that you should avoid or abandon your depressed friends. However, it is important to be aware if your energy is being drained by unconscious entrainment resulting from a sound or a person.

General Examples of Entrainment

Rod, a Harley Davidson motorcycle fan, explained that people who ride Harleys claim that, "If you haven't felt the hum of a Harley, you just don't understand." Rod related this conviction to entrainment, in that the motor of the Harley Davidson motorcycle has a special hum that feels good. (Since I have only been on a motorcycle for a brief moment, I can only conjecture that the vibration of the Harley's motor synchronizes or entrains with the human heart in a way that feels good!).

Marjorie, a woman at one of my seminars, related how her grandmother who loved to knit always brought along her current knitting project and knitted while people talked and other activities were going on around her. Several family members played musical instruments and loved to play together at family events. On occasions when the music got faster and faster, Marjorie's grandmother would soon knit starting at the same speed as the music. While Marjorie had always been amused at this phenomenon, she didn't have a label for it until she heard about entrainment.

Entrainment may also explain why people are drawn to great singers. Measuring the vibrato rates of famous singers, Dr. Harold Seashore in the 1920s and 30s found that the famous singer Caruso sang at 7.1 cycles a second, Galli-Curci at 7.4, and Martinelli at 6.8 cycles a second. These cycles per second correspond to a theta-wave state of the brain – the ideal brain wave for healing and creativity. Presumably when we hear a great singer who emits theta-state vibration, we begin to entrain and soon feel better ourselves because we are sinking into the theta-brain state ourselves.[7]

A more common experience with entrainment occurs in places where people have the opportunity to dance. When you find yourself in a place where there is music and people are dancing, have you ever noticed that your body wants to move to the music? Small children almost always move to entrain with music. Similarly, when we get older and have accumulated layers of conditioning and inhibitions about body movements and self-expression, we may still want to get up and dance with the music, because our bodies want to entrain with the music, but our inhibitions often stop us. Many ethnic groups hold celebrations where everyone individually dances to the music, entraining with his/her own rhythm.

In our mainstream culture we have strict rules about couples dancing together, i.e., male with female, which creates tremendous inhibition about following the body clues about moving or entraining with music. On the other hand, in celebrations or rituals where everyone gets up and dances together, it is much easier to entrain with the music and feel in harmony. I'm sure many readers can identify with this. Have you had the awkward experience at a wedding reception, etc., where there happens to be wonderful music, and you want to dance, but have no partner? Because your body wants to entrain to the music, you may experience frustration if there doesn't happen to be an opposite-sex dance partner available. Imagine yourself in a foreign culture where it is appropriate to dance alone or with the group and feel the difference inside. It is a much more natural feeling.

How Entrainment Can Improve Your Life

Entrainment also works with teachers and students. This explains why an apprenticeship works so well, because when you spend enough time with someone who inspires you, you begin to entrain with that person. This form of education is much more effective than just learning from lectures and books.

A successful trial lawyer, whom I'll call Bart, told me an interesting entrainment story. Part of the secret to his success before a trial consisted of an early morning ritual. Bart would get out of bed and immediately put on one of Wagner's symphonic works, much of which is perceived to be angry and aggressive. Bart would allow himself to be consumed by the angry energy of the music and even march around the house in time with the music until he could feel his blood pressure rising. According to Bart, by the time he had finished breakfast and was ready to drive to the court house, he had reached such a frenzied, aggressive state that he could win almost any trial!

But if he is unstressed then all those under him, even if they themselves are usually stressed by the act of performing, will rise above this in response to the pulse that he transmits to them, ensuring a high energy therapeutic performance.

Personally, I have experienced entrainment in playing tennis. For example, when I play with someone who is significantly more skilled than me, a rhythm often occurs with the volleying that is very satisfying. This is because a stronger player can set up a volleying rhythm that the weaker player will start entraining with. Needless to say, this is an excellent way to improve one's game.

On the other hand, playing tennis with a strong, effective partner who is more skilled than you, but is erratic in his or her game will not improve your game as fast because it is much harder to entrain with such a person. I often wondered why I liked to play with very steady players who could set up a volley and keep it going in a nice rhythm. Now I realize that it is because of entrainment that it feels good and that my game can improve in only a few minutes of play.

A man in the construction business who has a very busy schedule explained to me that he lives by a lake so he can get in his row boat after a hectic day. Entraining to the rhythm of the gentle waves on the lake is the only way he can wind down after a stressful fast-track day.

Aerobics classes are another place where the importance of entrainment is obvious. I once took a water aerobics class from a 22-year-old instructor who played heavy metal rock music for us to do water aerobics by. The average age in the class was approximately 40 years old. I found these rhythms very annoying and not in sync with the rhythms we were trying to achieve in the water. If the aerobics instructor had understood the entrainment theory she would be able to choose the background music more carefully to suit the rhythms of the students and the overall goal of the instruction.

In the realm of musicians, professional orchestral players have reported experiencing entraining with the conductor. A conductor with vital energy has the ability to make all the players entrain with her/him, thereby setting up a situation that makes the music exciting, not only for the orchestra musicians, but also for the audience.

> *In music, the miracle of entrainment is made explicit. The performer's every gesture, every micromovement, must be perfectly entrained with the pulse of the music, or else the performance falls apart. The conductor of the symphony can be viewed as an absolute ruler, but he rules by playing with – that is, becoming entrained with – his orchestra. And entrainment, again, involves no stimulus-response, no action-reaction.*[8]

While on the subject of this phenomenon, Dr. John Diamond points out that it is important that the conductor is not stressed, because otherwise the players would entrain to her/his stressful energy and convey this through the music.

> *It is essential that the conductor be unstressed during performance because if he is stressed he will interfere with the natural breathing of all the performers under him. This will prevent the free transmission of the pulse, the very soul and vitality of the music. But if he is unstressed then all those under him, even if they themselves are usually stressed by the act of performing, will rise above this in response to the pulse*

As the body rhythms go down, our ability to remember facts and figures is greatly increased. For example, in a group of people, ages 22 to 60, researchers found that after a single day-long session with the slow Baroque music, students remembered one thousand foreign language phrases, almost half the working vocabulary of a language.

*that he transmits to them, ensuring a
high energy therapeutic performance.*[9]

Entrainment and Improved Learning Abilities

Dr. Lozanov from Bulgaria developed a technique for greatly increasing one's learning abilities based on the premise that we are better able to function mentally when our body is relaxed; that is, operating at efficient levels.[10] Dr. Lozanov's method consisted of using relaxation techniques accompanied by slow Baroque music in the background. Baroque music in this style is approximately 60 beats a minute, which corresponds to a very relaxed heartbeat. Lozanov found that the rhythms of the body – heartbeat, brain waves and blood pressure – tended to slow down and synchronize with the beat of the music. Thus, the experimental subjects' heartbeats slowed by an average of at least five beats per minute. At the same time, their blood pressure was reduced and their beta brain waves slowed down to alpha waves, or 8 to 13 cycles per second.

As the body rhythms go down, our ability to remember facts and figures is greatly increased. For example, in a group of people, ages 22 to 60, researchers found that after a single day-long session with the slow Baroque music, students remembered one thousand foreign language phrases, almost half the working vocabulary of a language. In addition to remembering 1000 phrases they also had a 97 percent retention level. Dr. Lozanov says, "Human memory is virtually limitless."[11] These findings are significant because they show how slow Baroque music affects body rhythms and facilitates both the relaxation process and improved intellectual functioning.

In the book *Superlearning 2000*, the following story was reported about accelerated learning with music as it is being used in Japan:

In a large lecture hall at Japan's University of Tokai, four hundred engineering students sat breathing in sync. A soft tone sounded to pace the gentle rise and fall of their breath as their professor recited the day's lecture in an unusual rhythm. He drew from his own textbook, Electricity and Magnetism. *Eventually Dr. Hideo Seki put down his notes, the lights lowered and brightly colored diagrams came alive on a large screen. Soft music, Bach's Air in G, then Vivaldi's Four Seasons, began to play as the colorful slides, too seemed to march along in a precise rhythm. Not a word was spoken. As the last slide faded, four hundred students let their shoulders slump, felt their arms and legs grow limp and heavy as they closed their eyes and listened to special Baroque music. From a spot of warm comfort within themselves they heard their professor recite the exact same lesson over again, this time above the slow, steady beat of the music.*

At the end of the semester Dr. Seki, proved that this technique works well with large groups as evidenced in his published reports, "the number of students who scored high grades increased dramatically, while the number of low grades decreased."

In further support of using Baroque music for relaxation, a psychophysiologist analyzed the distribution of brain waves at different moments of relaxation/music sessions where subjects were gaining competency in foreign languages in two weeks.[12] Whenever beta activity or conscious activity increased, fatigue also increased. In contrast, when alpha waves, or dream-like states increased, relaxation occurred. Physiologists report that if one can reduce muscular tension, learning can occur at a more rapid rate. According to Dr. Barbara Brown, "With a slower heartbeat, mind efficiency takes a great leap forward."[13]

This notion is significant in the context of this book because expanded mental abilities during relaxation are important for the blood pressure training and other exercises. Increased awareness of one's body involves increasing one's concentration and intellect. It was discovered that the deep relaxation effects of the slow Baroque music were very similar to chanting, yoga and other meditative exercises.[14] The big benefit of the music is that you don't have to do anything in order for it to work! Your body responds whether you want it to or not. Coupling the slowed musical effect with conscious awareness only intensifies the results.

Another study showing the relationship between music, blood pressure, and improved mental abilities was conducted by Blanchard.[15] In his study, 254 students were divided into a control group with no music in the background and an experimental group with music in the background. The students were carefully matched on educational background, weight and emotional tendencies. Results showed a significant difference in pulse rate, blood pressure and test scores between the two groups. Specifically, the mean blood pressure of the control group at the beginning of the exam was 118/58. Three to four minutes after the exam it was 147/108, which indicates an acute anxiety level and an extremely poor recuperative power of the heart.

In the experimental group which listened to music, the mean blood pressure was 125/66 before the exam and after the exam, 125/69. Further, exam scores were significantly higher for the music group than for the non-music group. In summary, the group with the music background had dramatically lower blood pressures than the non-music group. Apparently, the music was also

I would sit at the piano blind-folded and get into a deep meditation and then wait for ideas. My fingers translated what I felt into music.

effective in reducing the tension levels, which also explains the significantly higher test scores achieved by the music group.

I designed a similar study using nursing students. During the most difficult test of their junior year, I played my 60-beats-a-minute music, *Mind Body Tempo,*[16] in the background broadcast over the intercom system. These nurses were only told that there would be a sound intervention during their testing period. A control group had no music during the same testing period. As in the study by Blanchard, the music group made higher test scores and had lower heart rates than the non-music testing group.[17]

After personally testing the 60-beats-a-minute Baroque music and satisfying myself that it really works, I began to search for other kinds of musical literature that work well for slowing the heart beat. One of my motivations was that about 30% of my clients resisted Baroque music, saying that they "did not like classical music" or that Baroque music "reminded them of an ex-husband," or some non-related person or experience. I decided to start writing new relaxation music at 60 beats a minute. I had learned the elements of traditional composition through the conservatory, but I wanted this music to come from the wellsprings of my creative unconscious. Therefore, I would sit at the piano blind-folded and get into a deep meditation and then wait for ideas. My fingers translated what I felt into music.

Athletes often came to my workshops seeking mental techniques to improve their performances. For example, they would say, "my heart beat is already slow. Can't you write some music at an even slower rate?" After hearing this repeatedly, it finally sunk in, and I went to work on a slower rhythm. I found it was very difficult to write music at 50 beats a minute and make it sound interesting. However, I finally came upon an idea after visiting a gentle waterfall near an underground cave with a huge spring. The water fell at about 50 beats a minute and the sound was overwhelmingly gentle. Afterwards, I started trying to reproduce this beautiful nature sound and rhythm, and nine months later, my tape *Deep Daydreams* was born. (Side one is exactly 60 beats a minute, side two is exactly 50 beats a minute).

You may wonder what is the difference between 50- and 60-beats-a-minute music. I have found that the 50 beats music has a more dramatic effect on the listener than the 60 beats. It seems logical that the scientific principle of entrainment would slow you down physiologically more rapidly, than the faster beat. This is usually the case, however, there are some people who prefer the 60 beats for relaxation. The 50 beats a minute can be scary to people who are not familiar with deep meditative states. There can be a sense of losing control when you feel your body start to entrain with the rhythm. It is important to tell yourself that in this situation, it is OK and safe to give up control and allow your body to entrain with the music.

The following chapter explains the techniques I have developed using specially metered music. There are exercises at the end of the chapter so you can experience this phenomenon yourself.

CHAPTER 2

ENTRAINMENT AND MUSICAL BIOFEEDBACK – HOW THEY RELATE

Applying the theory of entrainment, I developed the concept of *Musical Biofeedback*,[1] which uses specially metered music as a point of reference for helping individuals change their body rhythms. Adam came to me for heart arrhythmia problems, which he sensed were caused by stress, even though his doctor had prescribed a drug and did not encourage him to seek a natural cure. During his first session, Adam listened to 60-beats-a-minute music with his eyes closed while being told to focus his mind on his heart beating. I suggested that he visualize his heart in his chest cavity if that came easily, but that it was not essential.

After merely one session, Adam was able to feel his heart beat and monitor if it was slower or faster than the steady beat of the music. This gave him a sense of accomplishment and helped calm him at the same time. I then told him to notice if his heart beat entrained with the music. Adam reported that he could feel his stressed heart slowing down to entrain with the music. This observation was very exciting to Adam who had felt very helpless about his heart condition. The following is an excerpt from one of Adam's sessions:

Adam: OK, I can let go of the fear. It feels great to give my heart gratitude. I never thought about doing that, and yet it seems so natur-al now. Long overdue. It feels like the beat of the music is giv-ing my heart a rest. I can feel all my muscles letting go now as well.

Adam: *I can feel my heart gradually slowing to match the music. It feels really great. Frankly I didn't think I could do it! I can see my heart pump-ing blood everywhere. This scares me a little bit.*

Therapist: *Breathe deeply and look at your heart beating with appreciation. It is working for you. See if you can let go of the fear and just be the observer.*

Adam: *OK, I can let go of the fear. It feels great to give my heart gratitude. I never thought about doing that, and yet it seems so natural now. Long overdue. It feels like the beat of the music is giv-ing my heart a rest. I can feel all my muscles letting go now as well.*

When my clients have felt their hearts slowing to the 60-beats-a-minute music, then I switch to 50 beats a minute music. This slower pace music is usually easy for the client to achieve. Most peo-ple enjoy the slower tempo and feel a sense of accomplishment that they can use this tool to slow themselves down physiologically.

Sometimes the musical biofeedback sessions are strictly an exercise in slowing down the body and usually result in a deep sense of relaxation at the end. However, at times emotional issues are revealed. For example, Clarissa came for musical biofeedback because she suffered from rapid heart beats and an occasional arrhythmia. She could not pinpoint a cause, either physical or emotional. Everything in her life seemed to be in order and to be non-stressful. During her session she visualized a heavy dark cloud attached to the left side of her heart. Her heart beat started out at 90 beats a minute and dropped to 75 when she experienced this image. She reported:

Clarrisa: *I cannot relax because I see*

this cloud image. It is black and heavy. It will not leave. It is scary to me and I feel like opening my eyes to make it go away.

Therapist: *Try to keep your eyes closed and just be the observer. You are safe, and it is OK to watch and observe this black cloud. Breathe deeper as you watch the blackness. Can you see what is inside the black cloud? Give yourself permission to look inside.*

Clarrisa: *OK, I can relax now. I am trying to go inside. I am just hovering over it like a helicopter would hover. It is a little scary, but I am going to gradually lower myself into the cloud and see what it feels like. It is kind of exciting - a mixture of fear and excitement. Here I go. I feel myself back in third grade. I have my head on my desk and feel very dejected. There is blackness everywhere because I won't raise my head up in the light. I feel like crying.*

Therapist: *Do you know why you are crying?*

Clarrisa: *Yes, I can see myself being so excited to play volleyball and the coach rejecting me because I was too small and couldn't hit the ball hard enough. It feels so lonely to see my friends on the team, and me left out. I don't understand. I play at home in the backyard all the time. We play at the park and have fun and the other kids don't mind if I am smaller. Here at school it matters. I feel sad and very angry at the coach.*

Therapist: *Stay connected with your feelings. It is OK to express whatever you need to.*

Clarrisa: *I see myself getting so*

angry that I am able to unbury my head from the school desk. The anger gives me the energy to march up to the coach and say, 'I hate you for rejecting me for such a stupid reason. You should not be allowed to hurt children just because they are small. Winning is not the point. I see myself as a little kid, kicking him in the shins. He winces from pain and feels bad about what he did. I experience a sense of relief and power that I was able to hold my head up and express how I felt.

After this session, Clarissa's heart rate was down to 64 beats a minute. She felt a sense of calm after the storm and as she put it, "a new sense of inner peace." She explained that growing up she had experienced several traumas because she was smaller than the other kids and that it had caused much frustration. She had no idea that her rapid heart beat would uncover this child-hood memory. Yet it is common for clients with physical problems, such as a rapid heart beat, to end up releasing an anger memory similar to Clarissa's. Releasing these memories results in a return to a more normal heart rate.

In Clarissa's session it was important that she stayed with the black cloud image long enough to be able to confront it rather than continue to be afraid. Fear merely increases rapid heart rate and also creates other stress problems. In addition, it was important that she was able to inwardly express her anger to the coach. This turned her powerless feelings into a sense of power and over-coming and gave her a sense of closure on this issue. Now when Clarissa experiences a rapid heart beat or arrhythmia, she can play the music, match her heart beat to the beat, and feel in control of the situation.

Mental Activity and Its Physiological Effects

Visualization, when directly experienced, can be a powerful tool to help facilitate a deep state of relaxation and bring about attitudinal changes. Visualization is a means of internally changing the belief system.[2] When attitudes are changed or healed, the body responds by healing itself.

Some very innovative work in visualization was done by Dr. Simonton, a radiation oncologist who reported significant results with terminal cancer patients from teaching them relaxation and visualization techniques. As part of the technique, he taught subjects to visualize the healthy cells in their body fighting off the cancerous cells and disposing of them through the circulatory system. According to Simonton, the main characteristic of cancer patients is a poor self-image and a tendency to picture themselves as victim of the disease. In addition, the cancer patients who are able to fight back all have something in common, and that is the ability to "visualize themselves being well."[3]

Neurophysiological evidence has shown that mental activities affect physiological processes; in fact, mental imagery involving emotional topics can stimulate dramatic body responses. For instance, Meyer et al, found that alterations in blood flow through the cerebral cortex are associated with various mental activities such as thinking about pleasant and unpleasant experiences.[4] For example, if you think about a family member who triggers angry thoughts and you picture it in your mind, you are changing the blood flow through your brain. This study is significant because it shows the close interaction between mental imagery and physiological reactions.

Another researcher, Lang, has also come to the conclusion that mind-body interaction is extremely important in the development of disease or health in human beings.[5] In his "bio-informational

Lang maintains that mental imagery is not simply an isolated mental picture, but is thoroughly integrated with the physiological response system.

People with an ability to visualize mental images achieve greater physiological response during their imagery and, thus, are more successful in this kind of treatment.

theory," Lang maintains that mental imagery is not simply an isolated mental picture, but is thoroughly integrated with the physiological response system and can be experimentally measured. In studies, the people who were most successful in the use of psychotherapeutic imagery techniques were those who showed the most physiological arousal when exposed to imaginary frightening scenes. The least successful subjects showed very little physiological changes during their mental imagery, even though they expressed verbal fear.

One interpretation of this finding is that people with an ability to visualize mental images achieve greater physiological response during their imagery and, thus, are more successful in this kind of treatment. For example, if a patient attempts to control high blood pressure through visualization, his or her success is somewhat dependent upon the ability to produce more dramatic physiological changes; that is, stronger mental images in the hypertensive patient produce greater decreases in blood pressure, thus enhancing the healing effect.

The relationship between mental imagery and bodily responses was further illustrated in a study by Schwartz.[6] In his study, subjects who experienced feelings of happiness, sadness and fear through mental imagery demonstrated greater changes in resting facial muscle tension than if they just "thought about" happy, sad or fearful situations.

As indicated in the research reported here, mental visualization has a distinct therapeutic value. However, the ability to produce mental images may be waning in Western society. Constant immersion in a video-filled environment reduces our need and possibly our ability to elicit personal images because the need for visual thinking is diminished by such external stimuli as television, cameras, photographs and films.

Such dependence on external stimuli can lead

to a lack of creativity, a barren inner world, and stress-related diseases like high blood pressure. The more we focus on external objects, the less awareness we have of our internal processes. In my private practice specializing in music, imagery and relaxation for stress control, I have frequently observed this relationship between ability to produce images, internal awareness and general mental and physical health. The patients with lessened ability to produce mental images are the anxiety-ridden. Consistently, patients who can easily learn to produce images recover much more rapidly from stress reactions.

In summary, these studies show a relationship between mental imagery and physiological responses that has strong implications for the therapeutic use of imagery for treating physical problems. That is, if feelings of frustration dominate a hypertensive patient's thoughts, for example, s/he will simultaneously elicit negative physiological reactions. In a therapeutic situation, this negative thought pattern may be reversed by visualizing something positive and becoming aware of the subsequent positive physiological changes, such as lowered heart rate.

Motivation for Learning the Musical Biofeedback Process

Even though knowledge of one's internal processes is important for eliciting the relaxation response and learning to mentally control blood pressure and body rhythms, it is often difficult to motivate a patient to learn this process. Hypertensives know that high blood pressure has serious consequences, yet the majority still do not comply with their drug regimens because of the unpleasant side effects.

Because music provides stimulation to the brain's pleasure center, it can be used in treatment as a motivating factor. The music in relaxation/ awareness training makes the training more pleasurable, thus increasing the level of motivation and enhancing brain functions.

Therefore, a hypertension regimen that motivates patients to comply with treatment is valuable. Research has shown that a high level of motivation can be aroused by stimulating the brain's pleasure centers: Experiments "show clearly that brain functions will be enhanced if feelings are pleasurable."[7] Because music provides stimulation to the brain's pleasure center, it can be used in treatment as a motivating factor. The music in relaxation/awareness training makes the training more pleasurable, thus increasing the level of motivation and enhancing brain functions.

In summary, imagery/relaxation techniques and music processing are not isolated functions. Rather, they represent a synthesis that is intimately connected with the physiology of an organism. By applying these techniques in the treatment of hypertension, people's mental potential and their ability to control their body processes may be enhanced.

Reasons for Combining Imagery and Music

The techniques used in this book are an amalgamation of methods that have all been researched individually. I have found in my private practice that combining imagery, relaxation techniques and metered music has an additive effect on lowering blood pressure and/or reducing stress effects in general. For example, individuals who have suffered a heart attack are usually advised by their physician to get plenty of rest, eat a nutritious diet, and get proper exercise. One of these factors alone is not as effective in the healing process as the additive effect of all three. For the

People report being more attuned to body messages, and as a result, they try to do yoga or walk more in an effort to erase the small symptom quickly before it turns into something that is more difficult to cure.

same reason, adding music to imagery and relaxation is important to better be able to take advantage of the additive effect.

When you take a drug, you usually feel a powerful effect, which is often accompanied by some side effect. This is the price we pay for taking pharmaceutical drugs: we get quick reactions, but often suffer side effects. Further, usually these drugs do not cure the source of the problem. When you use more natural treatments, on the other hand, the effects tend to be more subtle, and it is often helpful to combine several methods to achieve quicker end results. Further, using natural approaches creates a more empowered feeling which is healthy – both physically and emotionally – whereas putting all the power into a pill can create feelings of hopelessness and a sense of "I don't have any control over my body."

Increased Sensitivity

One of the payoffs of practicing the following exercises is increased sensitivity. Many people have reported feeling more sensitive to their environment, such as being bothered by unpleasant noises they hadn't notice before. Also, people are more sensitive to how the food they eat affects their bodies. For example, many clients have mentioned that after this training they wanted to eat a diet more rich in raw foods – vegetables and fruits – and found themselves naturally giving up desserts and meat. One woman, Andrea, mentioned that she was more attuned to sound and how it affected her. This included throwing away records and tapes that she previously loved and now found abrasive. Also, people report being more attuned to body messages; for example, aches and tensions that they would have previously ignored. As a result, they try to do yoga or walk more in an effort to erase the small symptom quickly before it turns into something that is more difficult to cure.

Why It Is Important to Be Able to Feel Your Heart Beat

In working with cardiac patients and people with hypertension, I have found that most are not in touch with their heart area, which means that stress or tension is stored in that part of the body, making it more vulnerable to stress. By storing tension in one area of the body, we create a barrier or a numbing effect; therefore, in these situations, when asked if we can feel our heart beating, we are more likely to say, "No, I can't feel anything." If you belong in this category, you particularly need the following exercises as preventive measures.

Musical Biofeedback Exercises

The following are exercises to help you learn to lower your blood pressure, improve heart arrhythmias and generally increase body awareness. They combine music from the accompanying tape, relaxation, and imagery techniques. Practicing these techniques, which I call *music-assisted biofeedback*, will help you increase your sensitivity to your body rhythms and messages – they will help you become friends with your body. Failing to listen to your body, on the other hand, is abusive behavior. If you are not in the habit of listening to your body cues, make a commitment to develop a better relationship with your body, just the same as you would make a commitment to

We are constantly pulsating with our environment in an effort to attain harmony.

see a marriage counselor to improve a significant relationship, for example.

Understanding entrainment can be very helpful as a tool for slowing your body rhythms either for a specific healing reason or just to feel more empowered and in touch with your body. The stories and concepts presented in this chapter emphasize that we are constantly pulsating with our environment in an effort to attain harmony. However, along with this, the exercises at the end of the chapter will help incorporate the ideas about entrainment and bring them to your conscious awareness. Usually, this is an unconscious process. Experience is the best teacher. If you choose to explore these phenomena, try the exercises and see how they affect your body rhythms.

Failing to listen to your body, on the other hand, is abusive behavior. If you are not in the habit of listening to your body cues, make a commitment to develop a better relationship with your body, just the same as you would make a commitment to see a marriage counselor to improve a significant relationship, for example.

Musical Biofeedback Exercise For Heart Beat

Music to use: *Music With a Purpose* cassette by Janalea Hoffman, Side 1. Music composed at exactly 50 beats per minute specifically prepared to correspond with the following musical biofeedback exercises. (See enclosed order information).

Read the following directions before you start the tape.

- ▶ Take your heart rate and record it on paper.
- ▶ Listen to your heartbeat throughout this exercise and notice if your heart rate is in synchrony with the musical rhythm.
- ▶ Visualize your heart area. See if you can visualize arteries flowing in and out of your heart.
- ▶ Don't worry if you don't know exactly what a heart looks like, just let your imagination create the image.
- ▶ If you feel you are just seeing an image based on past experience, like from an anatomy book, don't worry about that either. **Trust whatever image you get and allow yourself to concentrate on it.**
- ▶ If you are *feeling* more than *seeing* an image of your heart beating, that is fine.
- ▶ If you are seeing an image of your heart and yet seem detached without feeling, that is OK too. Just be aware and make note of it later.
- ▶ Be aware if your mind wanders from the heart; gently push other thoughts aside and return your mind to the heart area.
- ▶ Remember to be aware of the rhythm of your heart beating and how it compares with the rhythm of the music.

You are now getting ready for the actual exercise. Sit in a comfortable place and make sure you won't be interrupted. For example, you may wish to take the phone off the hook, put a "Do Not Disturb" sign on your door, etc. Listen to side one of the tape in its entirety. After you have completed this music relaxation exercise, take time to answer these questions. It is OK to open your eyes and make a few notes if you think you might forget an image, sensation, or feeling by the end of the tape.

Now close your eyes and turn on the music.

Processing the Heart Beat Exercise

Could you feel your heart beating?   Yes   No   (Circle one)

When the music first started, was the rhythm of your heart rate:
- ❑ faster than the music?
- ❑ slower than the music?
- ❑ the same as the music?
- ❑ I could not feel my heartbeat

Was your heartbeat erratic at any time during the music?
Yes   No   (Circle one)

At what point did you feel your heart starting to entrain (synchronize) with the music?
- ❑ at the beginning
- ❑ in the middle
- ❑ at the end
- ❑ I did not feel my heart entrain with the music

When the music ended, was the rhythm of your heart rate:
- ❑ faster than the music?
- ❑ slower than the music?
- ❑ the same as the music?
- ❑ I could not feel my heartbeat

Could you also visualize your heart?   Yes   No   (Circle one)

If "yes," describe what it looked like: _____

_____

_____

_____

_____

_____

_____

Did you visualize your heart, but seemed detached from feeling?
  Yes   No   (Circle one)

If "no," did you see some other image? Specify: _____

_____

_____

_____

_____

_____

_____

_____

What was your overall feeling during this exercise? _____

_____

_____

_____

_____

_____

_____

_____

Did you experience any anxiety?   Yes   No (Circle one)

If "yes," describe: _____

_____

_____

_____

_____

_____

_____

Repeat this exercise once a day if possible until you can easily feel your heartbeat and are in control of your heart rhythms. The more you do the exercise, the more in tune with your body you will be. You will find that your experiences, feelings and imagery change. Documenting such change on paper helps you integrate your inner experience with your external life. If you practice the exercises every day, it is not necessary to put your answers in writing each time, but it is important to think about each question at the end of your musical biofeedback experience. You might want to keep a journal detailing your results.

Why You Need to Write Down Your Experiences Afterwards

This visualization exercise is a right-brain experience, which means it is inner-directed, creative, and feeling. Music is also processed on the right side of the brain, which is why music helps facilitate the visualization. Inner, or right-brained experiences are more powerful if they are integrated. For example, even the most wonderful experience may soon fade away if you don't write it down. Writing down these feelings is a left-brained activity. Combining the visualization and the writing creates a whole-brain experience. Whole-brain experiences are easier to integrate into your life than either merely right-brained or left-brained experiences. The physical act of writing the experience on paper may give you deeper insights into the meaning of the experience.

Musical Biofeedback for Breathing Rate Exercise

Music to use: *Music With a Purpose* cassette by Janalea Hoffman, Side 1. Music composed at exactly 50 beats per minute specifically prepared to correspond with the following musical biofeedback exercises. (See enclosed order information).

Read the following directions before starting the tape.

▶ When the music starts, concentrate on your breathing.

▶ Notice the rhythm of your breathing. Is it shallow, deep, erratic, etc.?

▶ Where is the breath coming from? Your chest, stomach, etc.?

▶ Does your breathing feel in harmony with the rhythm of the music?

▶ After you have felt your breath, see if you can visualize your lungs.

▶ Do they look healthy?

▶ Do they seem stressed in any way?

▶ If so, concentrate on the soothing rhythm going into the lungs to gently dissolve the stress.

After you have completed the music relaxation exercise, take time to answer the following questions.

Now start the tape and begin to concentrate on your breathing.

Processing the Breathing Rate Exercise

Did your breathing feel rhythmic and comfortable?
       Yes   No   (Circle one)

If "no," how would you like it to change?   _____

_____

_____

_____

_____

_____

_____

_____

Were you able to visualize your lungs?   Yes   No   (Circle one)

Describe the image you saw of your lungs: _____

_____

_____

_____

_____

_____

_____

_____

Were there any black spots or areas of stress in your image? _____

_____

_____

_____

_____

_____

Were you able to visualize the music going into the lungs and soothing any stressful areas?   Yes   No   (Circle one)

Describe how this looked in your mind: _____

_____

_____

_____

_____

_____

_____

Describe your overall feeling at the end of the exercise: _____

_____

_____

_____

_____

_____

_____

Musical Biofeedback for Blood Pressure Control Exercise

Music to use: *Music With a Purpose* cassette by Janalea Hoffman, Side 1. Music composed at exactly 50 beats per minute specifically prepared to correspond with the following musical biofeedback exercises. (See enclosed order information).

Read these directions before starting the tape.

▶ Relax as much as you can, allowing the music to help slow down your body rhythms.

▶ Concentrate on your breathing until you feel very relaxed.

▶ Now visualize the veins and arteries flowing through your body. You may want to use the metaphor of rivers and tributaries running through your body to help create an image of your veins and arteries. Imagine that you can see a clear picture of this process.

▶ Be aware of how the arteries look. Are they constricted or stressed in any way?

▶ If they look constricted, imagine that the music is relaxing them so that they slowly open up, allowing the blood to run freely and easily throughout your body.

▶ Imagine the network of arteries and veins in many different parts of your body.

▶ Do they look different in different parts of your body?

▶ If any of the parts look stressed, pause to concentrate on that area, allowing the music and your mind together to give a message to relax and to let go of any negative energy that might be stored there.

▶ Remember, if your mind wanders at any point in this exercise, just gently push the invasive thoughts aside and return your mind to the exercise. Do not worry if your mind wanders, this is normal and will diminish as you practice these techniques.

▶ After you have completed the exercise, take time to answer the questions below.

Now start the tape and begin to concentrate on your veins and arteries.

Processing the Blood Pressure Exercise

Describe how your arteries and veins looked in your visualization. Remember to describe the different parts of the body, if they were different.

Were they constricted?   Yes   No   (Circle one)

Were they relaxed?   Yes   No   (Circle one)

How did you feel during this exercise?   _____

_____

_____

_____

_____

_____

_____

Was this exercise easier or more difficult than Exercise #1 and #2?

_____

_____

_____

_____

_____

_____

If "yes," why? _____

_____

_____

_____

_____

_____

_____

Did your rational mind interfere? For example, by interjecting such thoughts as "I don't know what my arteries look like," or "What I am seeing just looks like something I saw in an anatomy book." This is a very important point, because if your rational mind doubts your image, it interrupts and discounts your experience.

Yes   No   (Circle one)

Evaluation of Blood Pressure Exercise

A client who went through this exercise of visualizing her veins and arteries reported having the following experience:

> I get an image of turbulence. I am getting an image from a movie I saw recently of a white water rafter having trouble getting through the rapids. I would say it is more of a feeling, though, than an image. The feeling is one of being over-whelmed. But since I watched the movie, I know he gets through. Just thinking about that makes me want to cry – that he had that much to go through. It took everything he had. It seemed like it would be almost impossible to breathe in all that water. But he made it out. He even made it through with his kayak.

This particular client was 38-years-old and was in therapy because of a problem in her professional life. She was in good physical condition, ate very little salt, and still had a blood pressure averaging 160/95.

Her imagery about the difficulty of the kyak rafter going through the water was a symbol of her own frustration at dealing with childhood abandonment issues. She stored these toxic childhood memories as constriction in the veins and arteries. After this session, she felt she had achieved a new insight into her body and how it stored old stress. She started practicing the musical biofeedback technique three times a week and was able to maintain her blood pressure at about 130/80 during the time I followed her progress.

As this example illustrates, these inner experiences help people understand what is going on in their bodies, which can be very helpful in changing the pattern of holding onto stress. For example, as I mentioned earlier in this chapter, body sensitivity and body awareness is a key to lowering blood pressure naturally. Most of us walk around unaware of what our bodies are doing internally. By using these exercises, you can change that old pattern and become very aware and, therefore, be practicing preventive medicine.

What Does It Mean If:

Your rational mind interfered? This is fairly common. One of the most important elements in making these exercises work for you is to *trust* your imagery, no matter how trite, insignificant or irrational it may appear. If it was not significant for you, you would not have seen or felt it. Use it as a starting point to go on to more meaningful imagery, or imagery that takes you deeper into yourself.

Your mind wandered. This is also normal. A lot of stress is caused because we do not have control of our minds. Minds that flit from one thing to another affect the body physiologically. Don't get discouraged, just simply see it as a warning that you need to practice these techniques even more.

You couldn't feel anything happening in your body. This happens sometimes when we are disconnected with our bodies. This situation will improve as you practice these techniques. Many people are so stressed that they have cut off feeling in their body. It is important to be sensitive to what is going on, so you can reverse the stress process. *Remember it is very dangerous to not be in touch with your body. This is how disease starts. If you are aware of your body, you can reverse the process before it gets too serious.* An example of stress taking us by surprise, is the story of the frog in a pan of hot water. If the water is gradually increased in temperature, the frog will boil to death because he is not aware of the gradual temperature changes. Don't be like the frog and boil to death from your own stress. Be aware of what is going on inside and outside your body. For example, people who have the challenge of migraine headaches, can learn to be more sensitive to early warning signs and thus ward off the encroaching headache or at least reduce the intensity.

You saw obstacles in your veins and arteries. This usually means there are obstacles of some kind there, such as cholesterol. When you practice this exercise, visualize the obstacles being flushed out of your blood stream. Literature shows that the body responds to images.

You cannot feel your heart beating. You may have stress stored in the chest cavity which makes the area feel numb. You need to keep practicing until you can feel your heart beating. You CAN get through the barrier. If you feel fearful of hearing your own heartbeat, that is another barrier that is important to overcome. Your heart is working for you, and it is helpful for you to visualize and feel it.

You cannot visualize. There are people who have trouble visualizing. If this is true for you, try to *feel* in the exercise instead of visualizing. This is usually a more subtle experience. *Feel* your blood flowing through your body, *feel* your heart beating, and *feel* your lungs pulse. Some people feel and sense rather than visualize. There is no right or wrong. It can be just as powerful to feel as to visualize images.

CHAPTER 3

MUSIC AND LOWERING BLOOD PRESSURE

Having explored rhythm in general and how it affects the heart rate, this chapter will focus exclusively on blood pressure and how musical biofeedback techniques can help you learn to lower your blood pressure. High blood pressure, or hypertension, can be caused by many different factors, both physical and emotional. Factors such as suppressed anger and resentment create internal pressure that can cause the blood pressure to elevate. If these emotions can be identified and released, often blood pressure levels return to normal.

Learning to lower blood pressure involves two major steps, developing more sensitivity to your body cues and learning to control your body rhythms. This chapter will focus on practical techniques to help you control your blood pressure. Specifically, you will learn how music can act like biofeedback to aid you in this process by matching your breathing rate and heart beat to the steady beat of the music, thus naturally lowering heart rate and blood pressure.

Even a frustrated or powerless inner child can be the cause of hypertension.

Your body is a rhythm machine in which many different rhythms interact constantly, whether you are conscious of it or not. Therefore, one of the keys to learning to lower your blood pressure is to increase your sensitivity to your body. Most people do not know what the ideal rhythm for their

*Repressed anger
can turn into
high blood
pressure, as in
Quinton's case*

heart is. As I discussed in Chapter 1, Music and the Heart, when you use music at a specific rhythm to help you slow down your heart rate physiologically, it gives you a point of reference. Having a rhythmic starting point is a key factor in the training process, which is why the correct music is so important.

Even a frustrated or powerless inner child can be the cause of hypertension. One example of this from my clinical practice is a man in his 40s, whom we will call Quinton, who came to me because he was concerned about his blood pressure which needed to be controlled with medication. In his therapy it soon became clear that his mother did not set clear boundaries for him when he was a child. Instead, she created tremendous anger in her son by repeatedly robbing him of his power and identity. One example of her poor boundaries was when, as a little boy, Quinton was given a beautiful birthday cake by one of his mom's best friends for his birthday party. Quinton's mom decided the cake was too beautiful for the children, so she bought them cupcakes instead and used the birthday cake for her own party a week later. This is an example of poor boundaries: the mother was taking a gift that actually belonged to the child. Quinton was not able to experience a feeling of self, since his mother would not allow him to have his own identity.

When something like the above scenario happens, repressed anger can turn into high blood pressure, as in Quinton's case. It is important to note that Quinton had no conscious memory of this event his entire adult life, until it came out in therapy. By bringing this incidence up in his therapy session, Quinton was able to feel the anger, not only from this event but from other childhood events which he had also suppressed.

We all need release valves for suppressed anger; otherwise, it can cause physical problems. Quinton practiced slowing down his body rhythms

We all need release valves for suppressed anger; otherwise, it can cause physical problems.

and reducing his blood pressure naturally by using the musical biofeedback techniques illustrated at the end of chapter two. Part of his therapy was to understand and face the truth about his painful childhood events, thereby releasing old pent-up energy in the form of anger, tears, or some other emotion.

I have found that when old feelings are acknowledged, we usually experience a significant sense of tension release, and our blood pressure goes down. Using the metaphor of a volcano for the suppressed anger, when the volcano blows, the fire and smoke come out, and the pressure is released. In Quinton's case, since 1990 when his blood pressure decreased due to new awarenesses about suppressed anger memories, he has not yet had to return to his blood pressure medication.

Another client, Clara, age 53, had the following memory in a music/meditation session, which enabled her to relate her hypertension to old childhood hurts. She related:

> *I can feel repression. As a child I could not make noise, couldn't shout, couldn't run, couldn't release any childhood energy. My energy has been tied up in knots because I can't give vent to it. I can certainly feel the power of that energy. I also feel my stomach being churned up. I could never say "no" as a child. I had no power and my mother spanked me without any good reason. There is a lot of anger about that, and it feels like it lives in my stomach.*

Pent-up energy manifests as high blood pressure. Clara's case also illustrates how high blood pressure can stem from unreleased childhood feelings. Clara stored anger in her stomach, which manifested in both stomach problems and high blood pressure. In her sessions she focused her visualization inside her stomach where she felt the pain and gradually remembered the memories above. After only a few sessions, she realized that her stomach pain related to childhood issues and she soon learned how to release the tension by using music/relaxation techniques.

Body Awareness and Hypertension

Medical literature refers to high blood pressure as an "insidious disease," implying that it is like a thief in the night who may jump out from behind a tree making you an unsuspecting victim. This attitude by some in the medical community indicates that we are powerless over our bodies. Many of my clients have told me that, despite what their doctors told them, they felt that their high blood pressure was stress related. As a result, I believe that many people with high pressure are noncompliant with their medication because they know intuitively that there is a more natural way to cure themselves. One client said,

> I have always thought my high blood pressure was psychological. It started after I got out of college. I lacked confidence in myself and was very uptight about my new job. I think this situation brought on the high blood pressure.

Another client developed high blood pressure after the birth of twins. She did not like children before she became pregnant, and felt overwhelmed and overstressed at the thought of caring not just for one, but for two babies. After practicing the blood pressure training presented at the end of chapter two, she commented that she felt better able to cope with her children. In fact, she now wanted to quit her job so that she could be home with the twins, whereas before the training she had mainly worked to escape the stress of being with her children all day long.

By becoming more sensitive to your body rhythms and following the methods outlined in this book, you can learn to feel when your blood pressure is rising. Blood pressure is a rhythm caused by the blood flowing through the veins. Once you learn to tune into this, you can slow it down when necessary.

What Is Hypertension / High Blood Pressure?

Various degrees of hypertension, or high blood pressure, are present in 23 to 37 percent of the adult population in this country. The effects of this disease are deleterious in that hypertensive subjects are a higher risk for heart disease, strokes, and kidney failure. In fact, hypertension is now the leading reason for doctor visits as well as prescription drug use.[1] However, effective treatment of high blood pressure reduces subsequent complications and, therefore, greatly reduces the risk of heart disease and other related diseases.

Hypertension, or high blood pressure, is categorized in two ways: essential hypertension and secondary hypertension. *Essential hypertension* has no known cause. Any person 18 years of age or older who has a blood pressure reading of 140/90 or greater with no known organic cause is considered to have essential hypertension.[2] *Secondary hypertension* is associated with an organic cause, such as a lesion of the brain, which is presumed to cause the elevated blood pressure.[3] This chapter is concerned with essential hypertension and all subsequent references to hypertension and high blood pressure refer to this type.

Until it reaches a critical level, high blood pressure is essentially an asymptomatic disease; that is, there are no outward symptoms or warning pain. Consequently, many patients do not take their prescribed medications, because they often have toxic and uncomfortable side effects. In addition, patients often do not keep follow-up doctor's appointments. As a result, the disease is extremely difficult to control.

Because of such poor compliance with otherwise critical treatment, alternative treatment programs must be developed. It is important, however, to establish a cause for high blood pressure before other treatment alternatives are designed. It is well established that stress, discomfort, and physical activity can contribute to high blood pressure; however, it is difficult to isolate specific causes in individuals. According to Harrison's *Principles of Internal Medicine*: "A specific cause for the increase in peripheral resistance. . . responsible for the elevated arterial pressure cannot be defined in approximately 90 percent of patients with hypertensive disease."[4]

In other words, high blood pressure appears to be stress related. It is difficult to study stress as a cause of high blood pressure, however, because individual responses to stress vary so widely. Selye discussed the problem of defining stress in the early issues of *The Journal of Human Stress*.[5] He maintained that it is difficult to study individual responses in large groups. Yet, the biomedical model for research is almost always a study of responses of large numbers of individuals to a stimulus or set of stimuli. This approach yields information about group-averaged behavior, but nothing about individual responses.

This vague response to stress was observed in a number of studies.[6] For example, parents of young children dying of leukemia did not respond similarly to stress; young men observed in basic training at Fort Dix did not respond the same to stress; and soldiers faced with a potential enemy attack in Vietnam did not respond in the same ways. Based on this evidence, it is important to consider individual differences when studying blood pressure management through biofeedback with music training.

The difference in the way we react to stress may stem from the way we perceive it. That is, potentially stressful situations are apparently perceived differently by different individuals. The person who perceives a situation as potentially threatening exhibits more physiological signs of stress than someone who perceives the same situation in a less threatening way. For example, people with high blood pressure who were given psychophysiological tests were found to experience more anxiety than the subjects with normal blood pressure, or normotensives, who were given the same tests.[7]

One interpretation of this finding is that a negative perception of a stimulus becomes manifest in a physiological stress reaction. That is, those people who viewed the psychophysiological testing as negative or stressful transferred this cognitive message to their bodies, which resulted in a stress reaction. On the other hand, those people who maintained a positive mental attitude about the tests, remained calm–both mentally and physically.

In studies in which both normotensive and hypertensive subjects were exposed to different stimuli such as (1) a frustrating task, (2) ice applied to the skin, (3) fear of an electric shock, and (4) anger from frustration caused by an irritating technician, the hypertensive subjects showed a significantly higher jump in blood pressure readings than the normotensive subjects.[8] The tests used an automatic blood pressure recorder that recorded the blood pressure continuously every one-and-a-half minutes.

This recording technique is significant because the continuous readings give a much more accurate accounting of the blood pressure than the traditional blood pressure cuff which interrupts the experiment. Immediately before the cold presser test in which the subject's hand was immersed in crushed ice, the systolic blood pressure difference was greatest. In addition, the family histories of the subjects in this study revealed that the normotensives who had a hypertensive history showed significantly higher systolic blood pressure and pulse rate than those without a hypertensive family history.[9] This experiment seems to indicate that blood pressure response to a mental stimulus (outside circumstance) is excessive in hypertensive individuals and that hypertensive family histories contribute to this kind of response.

In summary, the research indicates a relationship between stress and hypertension; however, hypertensives seem to perceive stressful situations differently than normotensives. If a relationship does indeed exist among perception, stress and hypertension, then an attitudinal treatment approach such as focusing on the causes rather than the symptoms is a viable treatment for hypertensive patients. The musical biofeedback exercises in this book help you gain a better awareness of your body rhythms and thereby the internal processes, with the result that you feel empowered to control your own body.

A common question about body awareness/music biofeedback training is how long the effects last. Since the training sessions I give take place only once a week for one hour, one might expect that any effects on blood pressure would dissipate during the week. However, the blood pressures often do not rise during the week even when no directives are given concerning practice, because many people who go through the training are motivated to practice on their own. One man said:

> *I use musical biofeedback at work. When a difficult customer gets on the phone, I just breathe deeply and things go much more smoothly. I really think my high blood pressure started at work when I would get extremely uptight with customers. Before this training, I could never relax at home or at work and I was constantly doing something. Now I am aware of any tension in my body and mind and I can sit and listen to music and totally relax.*

Another client who also practiced the technique at work reported:

> *I obviously can't sit and meditate at work, but after using the musical biofeedback training, I get more relaxed and think of my heartbeat and breathing, which makes me feel very stable and relaxed.*

My personal practice of body awareness/music training and my experience in teaching it to others has led me to the conclusion that the training is a cumulative experience. By *cumulative,* I mean that the more you experience a state of relaxation, the more it becomes a part of you. Individuals acquire reputations for being calm persons or hyper persons. These labels stick because of the sum total of that person's average behavior. The concept is similar to an actor or actress who learns how to be poised on the stage. If this poise is practiced enough, it becomes a pattern and is automatically transferred to other aspects of the actor or actress's life. As a result, when a good actress walks off the stage, she does not suddenly lose all of her poise, i.e., it is not an isolated experience. The poise becomes part of her character. The same could happen if you wanted to improve your speaking ability by joining a group like Toastmasters.

The same is true about meditative experiences. The more familiar you become with calm inner feelings, the more calm and controlled you become in all aspects of life. This effect is supported by results of a study where subjects were taught relaxation and their blood pressures were monitored continually throughout the day and night.[10] The nighttime lowering of blood pressure was greater than that expected by the normal daytime blood pressure variation; therefore, it was concluded that the nighttime lowering of the blood pressure was due to the relaxation training the subjects had received during the day.

In my work with musical biofeedback, I have found that in addition to clients' comments about deep relaxation and increased body awareness, some have reported transcendental-type experiences and increased creativity. For example, one medical professional commented:

> I felt God-like, very elevated – a subtle feeling of power. It was so different from usual levels of awareness or consciousness of the humdrum of everyday living.

Another client whose profession is engineering said of the blood pressure training: "This is a very creative experience. I would like to transfer it to my work."

Creative and transcendental experiences are very common in the anecdotal literature on various kinds of meditation and relaxation therapies. Using music as part of the process increases the creative aspect of the training because music is processed on the right side, the creative, feeling side of the brain, which helps people effortlessly get into their creative selves. In fact, of all the arts, music is the one that helps facilitate mental imagery more than any other.

The same is true about meditative experiences. The more familiar you become with calm inner feelings, the more calm and controlled you become in all aspects of life.

Reasons Why People Fail to Follow Through with Medication

The main treatment for people with high blood pressure is the use of medication that lowers blood pressure by chemically altering such physiological processes as the constriction of blood vessels. However, such medications also have potentially uncomfortable or toxic side effects,[11] including dizziness, dry mouth, fatigue, impaired sexual functioning, constipation, depression, nausea, vomiting, and severe diarrhea.

Because these side effects are highly undesirable and because hypertension does not lead to overt symptoms until irreversible damage often has occurred, many hypertensive patients do not comply with their treatment regimens. This lack of compliance and the lack of regularity with which many patients with high blood pressure remain under medical care and take their medication is a serious problem. In fact, the National Heart, Lung and Blood Institute estimates that fewer than one-third of hypertensive people in the United States have conditions that are under adequate control.[12]

In studies of patients' compliance, Caldwell studied 76 hypertensive patients who began an antihypertensive drug regimen at a Detroit hospital.[13] He found that one-half of the patients had dropped out of the treatment program in 11 months and only 17 percent were still undergoing treatment five years later.

Two other studies indicate that it is difficult to get hypertensive patients to keep appointments to even begin a treatment program. For example, Finnerty found that only 50 percent of hypertensive patients kept a follow-up clinic appointment during a Washington, D. C., population survey.[14] In addition, Fletcher et al. discovered that of all the patients examined at an emergency department in a hospital in Baltimore, only 58 percent of

Finnerty reviewed the records of 600 hypertensive patients in a small town in mid-Georgia. Sixty to 70 percent of these patients discontinued their treatment within two or three months. Similarly, in Atlanta, 100 physicians in private practice lost 60 percent of their hypertensive patients within a few months.

hypertensive patients kept their subsequent appointments at the hospital's clinic.[15]

In a second study, Finnerty reviewed the records of 600 hypertensive patients in a small town in mid-Georgia.[16] Sixty to 70 percent of these patients discontinued their treatment within two or three months. Similarly, in Atlanta, 100 physicians in private practice lost 60 percent of their hypertensive patients within a few months. Compliance is, therefore, low for both hospital clinic patients and private practice patients.

One factor related to low compliance is the complexity of the drug regimens, which often require several tablets per dose and several doses per day to even begin to achieve a goal blood pressure. Compliance also decreases substantially if effective drug regimens require a life-long commitment.[17] That is, if patients must take the drugs all their lives.

Another factor that apparently reduces compliance is that most hypertensive people are asymptomatic when they begin treatment.[18] An asymptomatic individual who feels considerably worse after starting the drug treatment than before does not have much incentive to continue the medication. The side effects of antihypertension drugs are probably the greatest deterrent to compliance. For example, one of the side effects of the antihypertensive drugs, particularly Aldomet, is impaired sexual functioning. This type of side effect creates a very stressful situation for a young male faced with this kind of treatment, for example.

Lack of compliance is illustrated in studies of the Hamilton steelworkers which revealed that when noncompliant, hypertensive men were asked in a nonthreatening way whether they were taking all of their prescribed medicine, 45 percent responded they were taking less than 80 percent of their antihypertensive medications.[19] In another study where men received follow-up care at the work site rather than in a physician's office, there was still no improvement in compliance.[20]

Compliance with treatment goes up dramatically when patients feel a sense of control and hope for improvement. Musical biofeedback provides this kind of optimistic opportunity. If you want to go through the techniques for lowering blood pressure, see exercises at the end of Chapter 2.

Earlier in this chapter, I referred to inner child issues that can surface as a result of the musical biofeedback training. The next chapter focuses on how music can help you contact that inner child.

CHAPTER 4

USING MUSIC TO HELP CONTACT THE INNER CHILD

uring a class that I taught on contacting the "inner child" through music, I asked the participants to remember a holiday that was significant to them. To help them relax enough to get into their unconscious minds where such memories are stored, I first took them through a relaxation/music experience. Then I suggested that they try to remember a significant holiday season and something they had wished for as a present. It could be a present that they had actually received or one that they had wanted but never received. At this point, the music changed from my tape, *Musical Hypnosis*, a very slow relaxation music designed to take the listener into the unconscious mind, to artist, Daniel Kobialka's orchestrated version of *When You Wish Upon a Star*.[1]

One of the participants, a 52-year-old woman, Shirley, remembered finding in the closet a doll that she was going to get as a Christmas present. She loved the doll, but when she actually got it on Christmas morning, she thought it looked grotesque. She described it as the most gruesome doll she had ever seen. She was very puzzled why it had looked gruesome to her. In this music/meditation experience, Shirley suddenly realized that she had projected herself onto the doll. Sexually

Music will enable you to see past facts to the very essence of things in a way which science cannot do.

– Vaughan Williams

abused as a child, she felt so bad about herself that she didn't feel she even had a right to live. Often in these experiences where one is in an altered state with the music, one image can illicit many feelings. In Shirley's case, the image of the grotesque doll represented the bad feelings that she had kept stored tightly in her subconscious. The music coupled with the deep relaxation helped her unlock this image which held so many bottled feelings. This was the beginning of a period of examining these feelings so they could be categorized, felt, and dealt with in a healthy manner.

Shirley originally came to me for therapy because she kept getting fired from jobs. She was very intelligent, but seemed to have a failure complex that manifested itself in behaviors that ensured she would be successful for a short time, but then always end up getting her fired. Also, in her relationship with her husband and children, she felt "used." Shirley recognized that her problem must be rooted in her subconscious, because she knew the problem was not because of a lack of intelligence, but rather a repeated negative behavioral pattern.

This imagery session with the music helped Shirley realize how her low self-esteem continued to be a result of her sexual abuse. Whereas one might think that dredging up this kind of painful memory so far in the past might be counterproductive, this realization after almost 50 years had a very healing affect. Painful suppressed childhood memories are like kidney stones. You may not be consciously aware of them or may not be able to see them, but they eventually have an adverse affect.

By bringing her subconscious memory to the conscious mind and working with it in therapy, Shirley began to see both herself and the doll as beautiful. What happened in the class was that Shirley touched into her subconscious mind where

In Shirley's case, the image of the grotesque doll represented the bad feelings that she had kept stored tightly in her subconscious. The music coupled with the deep relaxation helped her unlock this image which held so many bottled feelings.

this memory was stored, experienced the intense feelings, and realized on a conscious level what had occurred to that little girl.

Remembering her painful experiences and truly feeling the pain was like tearing down a dam and letting the water flow – a cleansing effect. Over a period of several months, Shirley's feelings of self-esteem began to improve, which became manifest in more success at work and not letting herself be taken advantage of by her husband and children. This happened as a result of her working with her inner images and allowing these old feelings to heal.

Shirley's story is one example of the role of the inner child or subconscious child that exists in every one of us. Our child within has a lot more influence on our everyday lives than most of us realize. For example, if we experienced traumas or didn't get our needs met as children, our inner child may be angry and hurt. These feelings can be so suppressed that we are not consciously aware that they exist. However, if your life is being sabotaged in some way in terms of relationships or your career, you can bet your inner child is kicking and screaming inside.

Painful suppressed childhood memories are like kidney stones.

The purpose of this chapter is not to teach you about the inner child in an academic way, but to give you techniques to contact your inner child in an experiential way. You can read every book on this subject, fill your head with interesting facts, but still have problems because you have never experienced your inner child. The healing comes when you develop a relationship that involves feelings and listening to your inner child.

I have developed some exercises, found at the end of this chapter, to help you experience your inner child and develop a relationship with it that will start the healing process. The following are some reasons why you might need to get in touch with your inner child:

> ▶ You have blocked childhood memories.

> ▶ You feel hurt or victimized frequently.

> ▶ You feel you are sabotaging your work but don't know why.

> ▶ You feel you are sabotaging relationships but don't consciously know why.

> ▶ You are depressed.

> ▶ You are irritable around children.

> ▶ You have problems with addiction.

> ▶ You have an eating disorder.

Why It Can Be Difficult to Communicate with the Inner Child

In contrast to children who are like psychic sponges that soak up all the feelings around them, adults can find it terrifying to contact the inner kid who is exploding with emotions.

If we were abused as children or our needs were not met in some way, such as not being touched sufficiently or not being allowed to express our feelings, our inner child goes into hiding and a false self emerges to protect the hidden vulnerable child. For example, a young child who is sent away to boarding school and longs for her/his mother may develop abandonment issues that manifest in addictions later on, because as a child, s/he was not able to protest or express her/his feelings about being abandoned.

It is difficult to feel these emotions as an adult. It is easier, instead, to develop defense mechanisms and denial so the feelings can stay suppressed. Of course, we pay a high price for suppressing our feelings. In contrast to children who are like psychic sponges that soak up all the feelings around them, adults can find it terrifying to contact the inner kid who is exploding with emotions. I have developed special techniques to facilitate this process. Music combined with relaxation/imagery techniques can be very effective at coaxing the child out of hiding.

Why Does Inner Child Music Work So Well in Communicating with Our Inner Child?

Music is processed on the right side of the brain where all our feelings are stored – both current and suppressed. More so than any of the arts, music is a powerful tool in creating imagery in the mind. This imagery combined with feelings is the key to unlocking powerful memories that create blocks to our personal growth.

Shakespeare eloquently stated why music is helpful in contacting the subconscious mind and retrieving buried memories.

> *Music can minister to minds deceased and pluck from the memory of rooted sorrow, raise out the written troubles of the brain, and with its sweet oblivious antidote cleanse the full bosom from the perilous stuff which weighs upon the heart.*

More so than any of the arts, music is a powerful tool in creating imagery in the mind.

Do you remember a time when you heard music and like pushing a button, tears came to your eyes? Most people have had this experience. You may associate the music with a particular event in your life, or you might not have a clue why it triggered such a strong emotional reaction. If the latter is the case, it is a strong indicator that the music tapped into a subconscious memory – you experienced feelings that bypassed your conscious mind. Often these poignant musical experiences are accidental, occuring because we happen to be somewhere just living our lives, not because we are consciously extracting the healing power of music and using it for our personal evolution.

Often the next step is to allow the feelings to make sense with your conscious mind. This usually requires a therapist's help, because we don't always want to know why we have those feelings.

Do you remember a time when you heard music and like pushing a button, tears came to your eyes?

In my experimentation with different kinds of music for contacting the inner child, I have noticed some clear patterns about what kinds of music work most effectively. Some of the very slow rhythmic music works well because the slow steady rhythms are comforting, just like being rocked as a baby, or they are reminiscent of rocking on a rocking horse or swinging on a porch or yard swing. Similarly, the steady rhythms are significant because they create a feeling of safety and nurturing. On the other hand, rhythms that change create a jarring effect that signals the subconscious to close back up if it had started to open to old memories. If we have suppressed childhood memories, it is because they are stressful; therefore, we need to feel very safe in order to recall any of the memories. The music can be a key element in feeling safe.

In one of the exercises mentioned earlier and also at the end of this chapter, I recommended using Daniel Kobliaka's *When You Wish Upon a Star*, which helps bring out memories, because the melody appeals to the child within and the beautiful orchestration appeals to the adult mind. If the arrangements are too childlike, the adult rational mind often rejects the music, which therefore doesn't take you deep enough into the subconscious to reveal any memories. The other inner child musical recommendations at the end of this chapter are based on much experimentation with private and group inner child sessions. For example, I have found that Strauss's *Till Eulenspiegel* is very effective at bringing out the playful inner child. The music has a humorous, almost mischievous spontaneity about it that hooks the child aspect of ourselves. You can play this music for a depressed person who is overwhelmed with their critical adult side, and ask them to listen and get in touch with their playful inner child and have a 90% success rate or better at changing their mood.

Examples of Different Aspects of the Inner Child

It is helpful to break down the inner child into various stages of childhood and corresponding feelings. What happens when you contact the subconscious mind is that you get in touch with different aspects at different times depending on your needs. By focusing on these different dimensions, therefore, we can get to the source of the problems more quickly.   Here are a few of the most common aspects of the inner child that people have reported experiencing in their music/relaxation sessions: Angry inner child, sad inner child and depression, powerful inner child, joyful inner child, wise inner child, playful inner child, 3-year-old who always wants help with everything, 3-year-old who wants help but always says "no."

The angry, the sad and the powerful inner child will be discussed in the following paragraphs. The other examples often emerge in sessions. There are exercises at the end of this chapter to help you get in touch with some of these aspects of the inner child.

The steady rhythms are significant because they create a feeling of safety and nurturing. On the other hand, rhythms that change create a jarring effect that signals the subconscious to close back up if it had started to open to old memories.

The Angry Child and Its Relationship to Illness

Pain or sickness can be a signal that your inner child wants your attention. The following is an example of a woman, Patricia in her early-40s, who had tumors on the ovaries and uterus, experiencing her angry inner child through music. The music selected for this particular session was my tape *Deep Daydreams*, exactly 50 beats a minute, to create a safe rhythmic feeling to help get to the source of the physical problem.

> *I keep seeing myself as a little girl, about five years old. I am seeing myself playing with my dolls. I feel like my parents are fighting and I am step- ping into my own little world with my dolls.*

I asked her, "Do you talk to your dolls?", and she replied,

> *Yes, I tell them that I am taking really good care of them and that I will give them lots of good attention. They won't want for anything. If I focus on them, I won't have to focus on the unpleasant things.*

In visualizing her inner child, Patricia felt the child adapting to the stressful situation in the household by focusing on her dolls and nurturing them in a way that she herself wanted to be nur- tured.

As a child, she had experienced a mother who was constantly physically ill or depressed, there- fore having very little time or emotional energy for her children. Patricia learned to cope with this and felt better about it by overnurturing her brothers, sisters, father, and even her dolls. This tendency to overcompensate has carried over in her adult life. She overnurtures everybody in her family and ends up being angry and ultimately sick when she feels unappreciated and used. When I asked her inner child to imagine going into the painful cyst area to explore, she responded,

> *It is very hot. I can hardly stand it. It is like fire. The cyst looks like a sore, tender place and I think it is sad.*

I asked her what the cyst wanted from her and she replied,

It is punishing me for when other people are unhappy around me. I feel like it is my fault and I am torturing myself for their pain. I hate my mother for not wanting me. This is why I feel this need to overnurture, trying to earn love, because I feel that if my own mother didn't want me, who would?

Patricia also exhibited symptoms of the sad child in this session. Often there is some overlap between the sad child and angry child. The inner child with music sessions usually focus on one emotion; however, it is quite common for the sad inner child to move on into the angry child. There is almost always anger behind the sad emotions. When a person gets stuck in the sad feelings without ever experiencing the anger underneath, depression and/or feelings of being stuck can result.

There is almost always anger behind the sad emotions. When a person gets stuck in the sad feelings without ever experiencing the anger underneath, depression and/or feelings of being stuck can result.

In the chapter on lowering blood pressure by means of music, I used the example of a man, Quinton, who found out that his inner child was so angry that he developed hypertension. In his case, his mother never let him have an identity of his own. This was the example of the mother who did not have good boundaries with her son which caused feelings of anger because the son had trouble separating himself from his mother. He was never encouraged to find his individuality, which created frustration that later resulted in hypertension.

Another case involves Raymond, who came to me for problems with facing reality and keeping a job. In spite of being very creative and intelligent, he kept losing his job and fighting to overcome an inner anxiety that he was unable to identify. In one of our music meditation sessions using a Bartok sonata, Raymond said,

*Now the music
is taking me out
of this angry
house and into a
Catholic church –
a cathedral.
I am sitting
there by myself.
It is hard to
believe that
there is a God
after all this
family turmoil,
and yet the
music convinces
me that there is
some kind of
higher power
with incredible
grandeur to it.*

I can identify with this piece of music. It seems like a voice is saying, 'that is you.' The emotional stress in the music is a reflection of my life and there doesn't seem to be any way out of it. I would like to escape this, but the music is taking me into my own inner turmoil.

When I suggested that maybe he could find a way out, Raymond responded that he was falling:

This seems like music to fall down the steps by. Wow, I made it. I fell down the steps into the big house that I spent so much of my life in as a child and young adult.

I'm running up and down the stairs. There is tremendous conflict there. Conflict over nothing. Everybody is angry – all my nieces and nephews, my mother and stepfather. Everybody is freaked out – angry about nothing.

I asked, "Are you angry too?", and he replied,

I'm angry at them because they are angry. They express their anger by brandishing belts and words. My stepfather likes to curse a lot over little things like someone didn't take out the trash.

Now the music is taking me out of this angry house and into a Catholic church – a cathedral. I am sitting there by myself. It is hard to believe that there is a God after all this family turmoil, and yet the music convinces me that there is some kind of higher power with incredible grandeur to it.

Comments on the Session with Raymond

This is an example of the power of music to take us into our subconscious mind where old childhood anger and conflicts are stored so that we can relive these experiences as adults in a safe environment. Raymond spent about 35 minutes imaging the turmoil and angry family images. He ended the session feeling that he was in a church where there was a higher power. This is a common occurrence with musical meditative experiences. Once the childhood turmoil is faced, there is often a feeling of going beyond the conflict – a sense of overcoming it.

Sometimes this sense of inner power comes naturally in the inner child sessions after some of the suppressed emotion is released. We will work on strengthening inner power in the last chapter.

Sad Inner Child and Depression

A 42-year-old woman, Ursula, came to me suffering from depression. In one of her sad inner child sessions, she gained some dramatic insights into her condition as she remembered something that had been stored in her subconscious since she was a tiny baby.

> *I am feeling hungry and getting a sensation of my mouth, and the idea of eating and throwing up – thinking about being a baby and not being able to keep anything down. Even a feeling of starving my body.*
>
> *I got the feeling of my uncle walking over and wanting to baptize me, but really wanting to drown me instead. I get this feeling that I decided I would do anything for my aunt because she is the one who could protect me from*

him. I gave all my power away as a tiny baby just to please her, so she would protect me from my uncle. It was all about survival.

Ursula had been abandoned by her teenage mother as an infant and left with her aunt and uncle. She experienced a lot of sadness as a result of this memory. This was an extremely significant session, because these preverbal memories are like crystallized energy that stop us from moving on in our lives. In Ursula's case, the memory had manifested itself as depression.

After a session like this, there is a need to keep exploring these feelings. Often there is a natural flow into experiencing the wise inner child or the powerful or playful child.

Powerful Inner Child

The following is an example of a segment from a powerful inner child session with a female client in her 30s, Sue, who suffered from severe depression. Her depression was caused from childhood issues, a divorce and a dysfunctional family. Sue found out that she was codependent and had learned to give all her power away to men even to the point of letting them talk her into sexual activities that she didn't want to participate in. She was powerless to say no.

We started the session by doing a relaxation exercise, then I put on the powerful inner child music and asked Sue to relax and start visualizing her own powerful inner child. She reported the following:

I see a little child skipping along the pathway who wants to feel important and be happy. She is trying to be happy. This child is by herself. She can enjoy her happiness by herself. In the presence of others happiness is not allowed.

This reflects Sue's codependency. Because there were no proper boundaries when she was a child, she has become so enmeshed with relationships that she feels she can't be herself or be happy unless she is alone. Sue continues:

She [inner child] wants me to make changes. She is a young, almost sexless child. Definitely not a little girl and definitely not a little boy, just androgynous. She is young but very wise. Definitely not naive or dumb.

I suggest that Sue ask the child what she wants.

I see the child in a room with sun shine and light – golden rays emanating from the child. The child feels like I have been giving my power away for too long. Just the child is in the room, but I have permission to walk in. The child and I are sitting down and holding hands. I guess I am just trying to understand that I do have this power inside of me. It feels really foreign. The child says I have been living for men for too long. I don't want to start living for my father through these men. Now I realize that since I wasn't close to my alcoholic father, I have become enmeshed with men to try and replace the father energy that I simply did not get as a child. The child seems to be sitting elevated to me like I am leaning at the feet of the child. I feel like I just want to walk away from the child and be by myself. I want to bring the thoughts with me and work with them.

I am walking along the seashore. I always wanted to live near the ocean. I feel a sense of peace and see endless possibilities. A sense of aloneness. This life isn't just for playing – it has got to mean something. All my life I have been searching for relationships but I want this relationship with myself. It makes me sad that I have neglected myself for so long.

I tend to get kind of childlike with men sometimes. It is really not like me to not realize my own power inside. It feels good that my father wants to protect me, but I don't want that either.

Identifying with the powerful inner child, Sue continues:

I see myself becoming my own woman, but I am not sure what that means. I see a great woman that I can become. It is like I see myself behind this big desk in a big office and I am in charge. I see this, but it seems hard like riding on a boat with many waves. Changes are hard.

This was Sue's first powerful inner child session. You can tell from her imagery dialogue that she is beginning to get a glimpse from a deep inner place that she has been powerless. But at the end of her session, there is a lot of hope and a vision of a different way of being. Usually when such a session is repeated, even greater feelings of power eventually become manifest in the person's outer life.

Most people who suffer from depression, chronic pain, migraines or other stress-related illnesses experience their sad or angry inner child first. Having dealt with these feelings, they can then move on to some imagery with their powerful child.

Summary

Often the emotional, inner child is the source of the physical or emotional problem. Earlier in the chapter, the case of Clarissa points out that she was sabotaging her success at work and at home and could not figure out why. Through her inner child, we learn that she was sexually abused as a child, which on a subconscious level led to her low self-esteem. By repeatedly sabotaging herself as an adult, Clarissa was fulfilling her unconscious belief that she was a grotesque little girl – not worthy of success or happiness. By finding and actually *feeling* the source of her low self-esteem through music, relaxation and imagery, her behaviors began to change and manifest more positive actions and feelings.

In the example of Sue who had difficulty with relationships and suffered depression, we helped her go to the source by experiencing her inner child who had learned to give her power away to men. By exploring these feelings thoroughly, Sue was able to move on to experience the more powerful aspect of herself.

Western medicine is notorious for not going to the source of various physical problems but merely offering Band-Aid solutions. For example, if you suffer from hemorrhoids because you eat too much refined food, such as ice cream, pie and cake, which is very bad for the intestinal tract, having an operation to cut out the hemorrhoids is not a lasting cure. Instead, when you go to the *source* of the problem by changing your diet to more intestinally friendly food, you can solve the problem more permanently.

As James Redfield points out in his best-selling book *The Celestine Prophecy*, we need to work through and resolve our childhood dramas. By going through the following inner-child-with-music exercises, you may get in touch with your inner child and discover more about the source of some of your negative behaviors or feelings. Our consciousness is expanded by getting in touch with our inner child even if we are not demonstrating any distinct negative behaviors. Besides, it can be a joyful, relaxing experience.

Exercises to Process the Inner Child

On the following pages are seven inner child exercises for you to experience. To be able to benefit from the exercises you must have the cassette that was made for this book, *Music With A Purpose*, side 2, the inner child selections (see enclosed order form). Sit in a comfortable chair, preferably near your cassette recorder, so you don't have to get up to put the music on. Make sure you will not be interrupted for at least 30 minutes. Just before you put the music on, tell yourself that you are willing to explore the child within you. I would suggest you briefly look through the following exercises to get an idea how you want to procede. Some people want to listen to one selection, turn off the music temporarily, and fill out the exercise immediately. Others want to listen to several before they turn off the music and answer the questions.

Tell yourself that you want to go to the source of your problem and, therefore, are willing to experience any feelings that your inner child wants to share with you. It is important not to shun these aspects of yourself, because by doing so you only stuff them deeper inside, which brings sadness, frustration, and confusion. Be compassionate for the next few minutes and listen to this child within who has been wanting to share feelings with you for a long time.

To best benefit from the following exercises, go through five or ten minutes of relaxation exercises before you start the music. Now you are going to slow down and take time out to listen and feel. If you don't get an image of your inner child, it is OK, you may just *feel* her/him. If you do get an image, notice where your child is – outside or inside. Is it a place that you remember or somewhere you have never been? How is your child dressed? What is the posture? Do you image your inner child coming close to you, or are you in the picture?

Now, turn the page and read the guidance for your first exercise, then sit back, close your eyes, relax, and start the music.

Remembering Gifts Exercise

For this exercise, read the following before you start the music. Begin to think about a time in your childhood when you had a wish for something. It might have been a gift on a holiday or just something you really wanted. It might be a material thing or might have to do with feelings that you desired. Visualize your inner child wishing for something. The music will help you get in touch with this aspect of yourself. Notice what kind of clothing your child has on and what age he or she is. If the imagery is not clear, don't worry about it, just get into the feeling aspect of your experience. If you find yourself feeling skeptical that you can go back to childhood, just relax and let the music lead you on this inner journey.

When the music stops, be ready to write down your responses.

Describe your inner child in this exercise: _____

_____

_____

_____

_____

_____

_____

_____

Who gave you a gift? _____

_____

_____

_____

_____

How was it given? _____

_____

_____

_____

_____

How did you feel about it? _____

_____

_____

_____

_____

_____

_____

_____

What was happening in your body during the imagery? _____

_____

_____

_____

_____

_____

_____

_____

What were the occasions when you received gifts? _____

_____

_____

_____

_____

Were there any gifts that you wanted, but didn't get?
     Yes   No   (Circle one)

If "yes," describe: _____

_____

_____

_____

_____

Other Comments: _____

_____

_____

_____

_____

_____

_____

_____

The Angry Inner Child Exercise

Did you feel anger?   Yes   No   (Circle one)

Describe: _____

_____

_____

_____

_____

_____

_____

Did you feel any resistance to the music? Yes   No (Circle one)

If "yes," describe: _____

_____

_____

_____

_____

_____

What part of your body reacted most strongly to the music? _____

_____

_____

_____

Did you feel like moving your body or making fists?
     Yes   No   (Circle one)

If "yes," describe: _____

_____

_____

_____

_____

_____

Describe any imagery you had: _____

_____

_____

_____

_____

_____

If you experienced anger, did you get a sense of how you could channel
this anger? _____

_____

_____

_____

_____

How old was your angry child? _____

Describe how s/he looked to you physically: _____

_____

_____

_____

_____

_____

How do you feel the music contributed to your experience? _____

_____

_____

_____

_____

_____

Other Comments: _____

_____

_____

_____

_____

_____

_____

The Sad Inner Child Exercise

Describe what you felt: _____

_____

_____

_____

_____

_____

Describe how you expressed your emotions: _____

_____

_____

_____

_____

_____

Describe any imagery you had: _____

_____

_____

_____

_____

Describe any resistance you experienced: _____

_____

_____

_____

_____

_____

Describe in detail how your child looked: _____

_____

_____

_____

_____

Did you have any resistance to touching your inner child or talking to your child?   Yes   No   (Circle one)

If "yes," describe: _____

_____

_____

_____

_____

_____

_____

Do you feel the music facilitated your experience?
      Yes   No   (Circle one)

If "yes," describe: _____

_____

_____

_____

_____

If "no," why? _____

_____

_____

_____

_____

Other Comments: _____

_____

_____

_____

_____

_____

_____

_____

_____

The Playful Inner Child Exercise

Describe your imagery: _____

_____

_____

_____

_____

_____

_____

What adults were role models for healthy play in your life? _____

_____

_____

_____

_____

Did you go back and relive any family vacations?
    Yes   No   (Circle one)

If "yes," were they playful?   Yes   No   (Circle one)

Describe: _____

_____

_____

_____

_____

What games did you most play? _____

_____

_____

_____

_____

_____

Did they always feel competitive?   Yes   No   (Circle one)

Did you remember playing with other siblings?
    Yes   No   (Circle one)

Can you remember dancing, singing or drawing without feeling
shame or inhibitions?   Yes   No   (Circle one)

Describe: _____

_____

_____

_____

_____

_____

How did your parents exhibit healthy play? _____

_____

_____

_____

_____

Do you feel the music helped you contact the playful child? _____

_____

_____

_____

_____

_____

_____

Other Comments: _____

_____

_____

_____

_____

_____

_____

_____

_____

_____

_____

The Powerful Inner Child Exercise

Were you able to get in contact with your powerful inner child?
        Yes   No   (Circle one)

If "yes," describe: _____

_____

_____

_____

_____

_____

_____

_____

Did s/he have on clothes?   Yes   No   (Circle one)

Describe: _____

_____

_____

_____

_____

_____

_____

_____

How old was s/he? _____

How did s/he manifest his/her power? _____

_____

_____

_____

_____

_____

How did this power make you feel? _____

_____

_____

_____

_____

_____

How do you feel you can integrate this power into your life? _____

_____

_____

_____

_____

Did you feel any resistance to the music or the exercise?
    Yes   No   (Circle one)

If "yes," describe: _____

_____

_____

_____

_____

_____

_____

Other Comments: _____

_____

_____

_____

_____

_____

_____

_____

_____

_____

_____

_____

_____

_____

_____

The Joyful Inner Child Exercise

Describe what your joyful child looked like: _____

_____

_____

_____

Describe how you felt: _____

_____

_____

_____

Describe any images you had: _____

_____

_____

_____

_____

_____

_____

Was s/he hard to contact?   Yes   No   (Circle one)

If "yes," do you know why? _____

_____

_____

_____

How did your body feel? _____

_____

_____

_____

How old was your joyful child? _____

Describe what s/he looked like: _____

_____

_____

_____

_____

_____

_____

Other comments? _____

_____

_____

_____

_____

_____

_____

_____

The Wise Inner Child Exercise

Describe how you saw your wise inner child: _____

_____

_____

_____

_____

_____

_____

Was it difficult getting in touch with her/him?
    Yes   No   (Circle one)

Was it difficult talking together?   Yes   No   (Circle one)

Did you do all the talking?   Yes   No   (Circle one)

Did your wise inner child do all the talking?   Yes   No   (Circle one)

Did s/he give any advice?   Yes   No   (Circle one)

Describe: _____

_____

_____

_____

_____

_____

If "yes," did you trust the advice? _____

Was there any emotion associated with the experience?
       Yes   No   (Circle one)

Describe: _____

_____

_____

_____

_____

_____

_____

_____

Do you feel like you can have access to your wise inner child again?
       Yes   No   (Circle one)

If "no," explain: _____

_____

_____

_____

_____

_____

_____

Other Comments: _____

_____

_____

_____

_____

_____

_____

_____

_____

_____

_____

_____

_____

_____

_____

_____

_____

_____

_____

_____

_____

_____

_____

_____

MUSIC AND CODEPENDENCY

The sounds in your environment and the lyrics to the songs you listen to are just as important as the food you put in your body. Given the nature of music and sounds, therefore, it is essential that we pay careful attention to the effect they have on our well being. Is the music in your world helping you move forward in a positive way, or is it helping keep you stuck in old patterns? This chapter will explore the idea of codependency and how popular song lyrics promote and/or reinforce feelings and behaviors.

What Is Codependency?

Codependency refers to a person who is so other-oriented that his or her life is affected adversely. For example, the codependent person feels powerless much of the time, relationships are not working, s/he suffers from addictions or has a number of physical problems.

When individuals come to me for relaxation training sessions using music, they are often prompted by some kind of physical complaint. Over the years I've learned that the source of the pain or stress often lies in a codependency problem. For example, if somebody complains of a recurring headache, stomachaches, or sexual problems, I find that these initial symptoms are hardly ever the real problem.

A woman in her mid-thirties, Priscilla, came to me with stomach tension. In her session she used my tape *Deep Daydreams* – music at exactly 50 beats a minute – to achieve a deep state of relaxation. At the same time, I directed her to imagine going inside her stomach to the source of the pain. As a result, Priscilla reported experiencing the following imagery and feelings:

> *It is pulsating, things are hitting each other – dark, chaotic things. I don't want to go in. It feels like a really hostile environment. There is so much pain. I feel it is a lot of my mother's pain. I realize now that I feel responsible for a lot of her pain.*

Feeling responsible for a parent's pain is common among adult children of alcoholics or children from dysfunctional families. This is another example of a codependency problem. Because the problem is not conscious, the repressed feelings have turned into a physical problem. The technique used here of going within ourselves with the help of the music helps us realize that our physical symptoms are really left-over repressed childhood feelings or codependent problems. Once we actually *feel* this internally, we are motivated to work on the problem at a deeper level.

Because these feelings can be so painful, most people use the defense mechanism of denial to suppress them – usually leading to physical pain. A stomachache or migraine is more socially acceptable to talk about than emotional pain. Imagine calling into work and saying, "I have terrible emotional pain today, I can't come to work." This would not be accepted or tolerated, so we turn the feeling into something else.

Is the music in your world helping you move forward in a positive way, or is it helping keep you stuck in old patterns?

A stomachache or migraine is more socially acceptable to talk about than emotional pain. Imagine calling into work and saying, "I have terrible emotional pain today, I can't come to work."

Examples of codependency are all around us if we just open our eyes. I recently saw a talk show that focused on couples who had been dating for a long time. The women wanted a commitment, while the men did not. The comments by the men and women on the show made great examples of codependent statements. Some of the women made comments like, "I have done everything for him for four years and he still won't marry me," or "I just can't get him to give me a ring." This is a very manipulative, controlling attitude. Giving a ring may be ideal when done voluntarily – not when someone is trying to get you to do it.

Another young woman on the show said, "I've given him my life for six years and he doesn't appreciate it." This illustrates the caretaker syndrome that codependents so often get into – taking care of someone else while neglecting their own needs. After years of nurturing someone else, it is common for codependents to be angry that the recipients don't appreciate them.

One of the guys on the show noted, "Well, she is hard enough to deal with. If I give her a ring, what will she be like?" The man was really saying that he was not satisfied with the relationship and didn't feel safe to make a commitment. The woman was not hearing his feelings because all she could think about was fulfilling her own desire to have a ring. So, by caretaking, manipulating and at the same time failing to hear each other, the two were immobilized in their relationships. In these cases, the women were blaming the men because they wouldn't make a commitment, when in fact the real issue goes deeper than that.

Another classic example of codependency is apparent in the relationship of a couple, Allison and Harry, who have been married for 10 years. For the past two years they have been on a rocky ride in their marriage. Until this time, Harry had been the stable wage earner. After losing his job through a company cutback, he decided to take time to smell the roses, go back to school and explore what he really wanted to do. Allison panicked and became very angry. She began to complain about Harry to everyone who would lend an ear, started to talk about wanting to move across the country, and went on frequent trips. However, although constantly complaining about needing more space or freedom in the marriage, while away on a trip Allison would call her husband at least once a day.

When Harry offered her half their assets and her freedom, Allison refused. This type of conflicted behavior is a sign of codependency, or the "I love you, hate you, need you syndrome." After two years of tolerating this inconsistent behavior, Harry began to get more and more angry. Both were in denial about the problems in their marriage. What they were really complaining about was not the real issue. They kept calling it a difficult time in their lives, not recognizing it as a codependency problem.

When one or both partners complain a lot about their marriage but are unwilling to do something about it, they are facing a codependency problem. Allison and Harry's story shows two people living together: One complains a lot, but takes no steps to better the situation. If the wife came to me complaining about her husband losing his job and not trying hard enough to get another job, although the bills were being paid, I would consider the complaints a symptom of a bigger problem in the woman's life – her dependence on her husband! Rather than her own sense of powerlessness in the marriage, she is focusing on him. This type of other-orientedness is one sign of codependence.

Married people who constantly go to self-improvement classes or seminars and read all the right books and still have bad marriages or complain frequently usually have a codependent marriage. It is difficult to define codependency because it operates on many levels and manifests itself in various symptoms. For example, the person who repeatedly marries a chemically dependent person may be labeled codependent, but that is just one manifestation of this phenomenon. Anyone who has low self-esteem, lots of anger, or the caretaker personality, also fits the category. Codependency is also characterized by denial about our first family's problems.

Melody Beattie, author of the best-selling book, *Co-Dependent No More,* defines codependency: "A codependent person is one who has let another person's behavior affect him or her, and who is obsessed with controlling that person's behavior."

How Codependency Relates to Music

We are conditioned by the world around us, which is why we are codependent in the first place. It all started from dysfunctional families and the messages we received about ourselves. When codependency is reinforced by other institutions, people, and even music on the radio, it makes it harder to overcome. Thus, codependency is perpetuated by the lyrics of songs. Many love songs are full of the idea that "I can't live without you," or "I am nothing without you," etc. These lyrics sink into our subconscious minds where they perpetuate the problem.

Does this mean that you can't enjoy these songs? No! But it means that you must be aware, pay attention to what you are listening to, and realize that it may perpetuate old and dysfunctional belief systems.

Music is processed on the right side of the brain – the emotional, creative, unconscious side. Learning through rhymes and songs is very powerful because it engages the right side of the brain. An example of the power of music and the right brain is the alphabet song, which almost everyone can remember. While this particular song is very positive and instructional, songs that promote ideas that are not healthy stick equally in the subconscious mind.

Many love songs are full of the idea that "I can't live without you," or "I am nothing without you," etc. These lyrics sink into our subconscious minds where they perpetuate the problem.

A client of mine, Bob, has addiction problems to drugs and alcohol. He explained to me that when he hears Eric Clapton's song *Cocaine*, it makes him want to get in his car and drive very fast, go to bars, drink and get into old painful behaviors even though these behaviors never brought him any joy, only more pain. It is important to realize the power of song and song lyrics so that we can use it in positive ways in our lives. Bob did not realize this particular song affected him negatively until he took the *Music Diagnostic Self-Test* (found at end of this chapter) and analyzed his behavior. Answering the questions on the test, he realized that the Eric Clapton song was a trigger for old addictive behaviors.

The great English novelist Joseph Conrad once wrote, "Music has a 'magic suggestiveness' that reaches the secret spring of responsive emotions." Most people can remember a time when this applied to them. For example, can you remember standing in a department store and hearing a song that touched you and made your day seem brighter? Have you heard a song in church that brought tears to your eyes without you knowing why? There is a hymn called *In The Garden* that was my grandmother's favorite hymn and, therefore, was played at her funeral. She died when I was nine years old, and I have only one visual memory of her funeral. However, whenever I hear that hymn it brings tears to my eyes. No memory is attached to the tears, just deep emotion. There is no rational explanation for this except that we know music taps into the emotional side of the brain and that no one is immune to this phenom-

"Music has a 'magic suggestiveness' that reaches the secret spring of responsive emotions."

enon. You might search your memory for similar emotional responses to music and find that when you reflect upon your responses, an insight about your past is revealed to you.

The fact that music brings up old forgotten memories brings to mind the theory that memories are stored in the body. Music can be the catalyst that taps into these memories. The following account details how one professional has studied the effect of music on our muscular system. Researcher, medical doctor, John Diamond, has written several books about the power of music in our lives. He is well known for research and therapy work in the field of behavioral kinesiology – the science of muscle testing – which determines how outside energies are affecting our muscles. In his book, *Your Body Doesn't Lie,* he says:

> *Surrounded by the right sounds, we all can be invigorated, energized, and balanced. It has been demonstrated clinically that music adds to our general health and well-being. Music, then, can be an important part of our program of primary prevention – the prevention of illness at the pre-physical, energy-imbalance level.*

Based on extensive testing on the effects of music on our muscles, Dr. Diamond has found that 50% of rock music has an anapestic beat (da-da-DA), which is the exact opposite of a normal heart beat (DA, DA, da). A rhythm going against your normal heart rhythm weakens your muscles because your body has to work harder to counteract a foreign rhythm. After doing extensive muscle testing while individuals listened to different kinds of music, he reports:

> *Using hundreds of subjects, I found that listening to rock music frequently*

causes all the muscles in the body to go weak. The normal pressure required to overpower a strong deltoid muscle in an adult male is about 40 to 45 pounds. When rock music is played, only 10 to 15 pounds is needed.

Every major muscle of the body is related to an organ. This means that all the organs of our body are being affected by a large proportion of the popular music to which we are exposed each day. If we add up the hours of radio play throughout the world, we can see how enormous a problem this is.

The cumulative effect of the rhythm, the lyrics and the music is cause for concern. Being aware of the music in our environment and its potentially negative effects on our health, therefore, is as important as watching out for polluted air and junk food.

Addiction to Chaotic Sound

Another manifestation of codependency is addictions. We frequently hear about food, alcohol and drug addictions, but what about chaotic sound addictions? Rock music that weakens our muscles can be an addiction just like drugs weakening our bodies and psyche. Also, we can become addicted to codependent song lyrics separate from or in addition to chaotic sound. When I worked in mental health clinics, I found that many depressed people expressed a strong preference for the blues. The lyrics were depressing and tended to match their moods rather than uplift.

How do you know if you are addicted to chaotic music? Notice what kind of music you tend to listen to on the radio or what kind of music you buy. Are you the kind of person who has to have a radio or TV on all the time in your house or work environment? If so, you may be addicted to the sound so that you don't have to listen to your own inner voice. At the end of this chapter there is a *Musical Diagnostic Self-Test* you can take if you are interested in finding out more about the meaning and patterns of your musical listening behavior.

Core Symptoms Of Codependency

In her best-selling book, *Facing Codependency*, Pia Mellody lists five core symptoms of codependency. Along with Mellody's symptoms, I have listed the corresponding manifestations. Song lyrics that relate to and perpetuate these ideas are also discussed.

Core Symptom	Manifestation
Difficulty experiencing appropriate levels of self-esteem	Giving your power away
Difficulty setting functional boundaries	Poor boundaries
Experiencing and expressing our reality moderately	Denial
Difficulty owning our own reality	Looking for love outside of ourselves
Difficulty acknowledging and meeting our own needs and wants	Dependency and/or caretaking

Giving Your Power Away

One of the most significant symptoms of code-pendency is giving your power away to other people, especially lovers. Because of low self-esteem we externalize our power by projecting it onto others. An example of a song promoting this phenomenon is *Only You*, which is on Reba McIntire's album *The Best of Reba McIntire.*[1]

Only You

Only you, can make this world seem bright,
Only you, can make the darkness bright.

Only you and you alone can thrill me like
you do and fill my heart with love for only you.

Only you can make this change in me
For it is true, you are my destiny.

"Only you, can make this world seem bright," really says that I am nothing without you. With that conviction, think how this kind of person would be devastated when a relationship broke up. Hearing this kind of song and thinking such so-called romantic thoughts over and over sets the individual up for a lifetime of giving away personal power and never developing a strong sense of self.

In a music imagery session with a client, Madison, who had come to me with stomach problems, I asked her to image her stomach. Her response was,

> *I just see a big empty cavern. It is very depressing in here. I feel very sad because it is so big and empty and very dark. I can't believe how empty I feel.*

This is a case of someone who came in with a stomach ulcer, but was out of touch with her own sadness until she got inside her stomach and discovered her emptiness. This scenario relates to the above song because the person who feels empty inside doesn't have high self-esteem or a sense of power over their own life. She needs another person to complete herself.

Madison and I worked for weeks on getting in touch with the emptiness inside, and grieving about it. The next step was for her to visualize filling her stomach up with light or love to help increase her self-esteem by working on filling herself up and nurturing herself rather than receiving her nurturing through outside relationships. As a result, she felt better about herself, which in turn helped heal her ulcer because she was no longer bottling up her sadness by keeping it confined to her stomach. In other words, she was able to release her emotion, which made her feel better physically.

Madison felt better emotionally because she was working at filling herself up and nurturing herself rather than having to get all of her nurturing from a lover. Improvement in her relationships was strong evidence that her work was paying off. She felt the benefits were well worth the effort.

This could only happen when she was no longer desperately looking for someone to complete her. In her relationships, Madison was now a whole person looking for a whole person, which has a much better outcome than two half people depending on each other for completion.

Her new awareness about listening to these kind of songs has helped Madison think differently when she hears codependent lyrics. For example, she now substitutes "higher power" for the male character in songs that promote the idea "I can't live without you." This is her way of continuing to enjoy the music without letting the words send a negative message to her subconscious. If you like this idea, you can substitute whatever word works for your particular belief system; for example, instead of higher power, you could use God, Goddess, Jesus, etc.

Now that you have heard Madison's story, you may want to read the lyrics of *Only You* again and see if you interpret them with new eyes!

Exercise: Giving Your Power Away

Think of any song lyrics that you listen to or have heard that reflect giving your power away to a lover or spouse. Try to recall a song that has been important in your life and how you feel about its lyrics. When you recall the song, be sensitive to what it does to you emotionally.

Song title: _____

_____

_____

_____

Explain how the song sent you a negative message: _____

_____

_____

_____

_____

_____

Do you feel you internalized the message from the lyrics?   Yes   No   (Circle one)

If you circled "yes," explain: _____

_____

_____

_____

_____

_____

_____

Poor Boundaries

A lyrical example of poor boundaries is found in a song entitled *Upside Down,* made popular by singer Diana Ross.[2] Allowing another person to treat us badly or invade our space, is a symptom of poor boundaries. This song also reflects another symptom of codependency – equating love with pain.

Upside Down

Upside Down, boy you turn me
Inside out and round and round.
Upside down boy you turn me
Inside out and round and round.
I cherish the time with you.
Respectfully I say to thee
I am aware that you are cheatin,
but no one makes me feel like you do.

I know you have charm and appeal
I know you play the field.
I'm crazy to think you are mine.
As long as the sun continues to shine,
There is a place in my heart for you.

This song has a driving staccato rhythm, making it sound a lot like a carnival ride. It reflects the type of masochistic relationships in which many people find themselves involved. In other words, they are crazy about someone who treats them badly. The pain and turmoil of the relationship are expressed in the repetitive refrain, "turning upside down, inside out," while the singer still affirms she cannot give up the lover.

This conflicted situation is typical of codependents who due to low self-esteem create relationships in which they are treated badly – the only kind of commitment that seems possible to them. It is interesting how the song, *Upside Down*, expresses the pain of an unfaithful lover, yet assumes an attitude of "you make me feel so good." The person singing is no doubt reliving her painful childhood characterized by the message, "I love you one minute and slap you the next." Sadly, conflicting messages from parents are very common in dysfunctional relationships.

Exercise: Poor Boundaries

List a song that reflects poor boundaries:

_____

_____

_____

Explain how the song sent you a negative message: _____

_____

_____

_____

Do you feel you internalized the message from the lyrics?   Yes   No   (Circle one)

If you circled "yes," explain: _____

_____

_____

_____

_____

_____

Denial

Another popular song that reflects codependency issues, in this instance, denial, has the following refrain: "It must be rain drops falling from my eyes because a man ain't supposed to cry." That is, I will pretend that these are raindrops because I was taught not to feel anything, especially not to show my feelings. This kind of denial makes it very difficult to build healthy relationships. While this can happen with men or women, it is more common with men, since they are conditioned from childhood more than women to stuff their feelings.

I recently witnessed a grandmother saying to her two-year-old grandson who was crying, "I don't want to have my grandson crying on this videotape." There was clear discomfort on the grandmother's part with the emotion being expressed. What a message to start getting when you are only two years old, – don't cry, and particularly don't show your emotions to the family! A more healthy and compassionate way of handling the situation would have been for the grandmother to comfort the baby and try and find out why he was crying.

Another popular song that hit #1 on the charts is *How Am I Supposed to Live Without You*, by Michael Bolton.[3] The song starts with a classic denial statement:

How Am I Supposed to Live Without You

I could hardly believe it when I heard
the news today.
I had to come and get it straight from you.
They said you are leavin'
Someone's swept your heart away.
From the look upon your face I see it's true.

Codependents are so caught up in their need for love and dependency that they are often in denial about what is really going on in the relationship. Consequently, when one partner suddenly leaves as in this song, we often find a victim-like declaration of surprise. This shows denial because there are always warning signs in a faltering relationship. For example, the one who left would have been giving verbal or non-verbal hints that the other person refused to hear or see, whether consciously or unconsciously.

The chorus line of the same song is a classic reflection of both dependency and giving away power:

Tell me how am I supposed to live without you,
Now that I've been lovin' you so long?
How am I supposed to live without you?
And how am I supposed to carry on
When all that I've been living for is gone?

Taking these lyrics literally, think how boring and empty a person is when his or her entire life revolves around one person!

Looking for Love Outside Ourselves

Many codependents are depressed because they are constantly looking for happiness outside themselves. It can be a healthy experience to fall in love if you are a whole person; however, if you are feeling depressed because you don't have a lover on your arm, it may be a sign of codependency to feel like you can only come alive through another person.

Start eliminating the things you do that don't bolster your self-esteem. Weed your garden, so to speak!

Rather than looking for love outside ourselves, it is healthier to feel alive with other aspects of life. Do you ever feel a similar kind of excitement about your work, a hobby, etc.? If not, you may have some work to do in bolstering your self-esteem. For example, you can increase your self-esteem by getting in touch with what you like or desire, separate from your partner or lover's desires. Make a resolution to do some things just for yourself. If you end up watching football every Monday night with your spouse or lover and wake up one Tuesday morning and realize that you really hate football, it is time to do something that *you* like to do. You can communicate this realization to your significant other and perhaps negotiate other activities together, or simply go do your own thing.

Another way to bolster your self-esteem is by being brutally honest with yourself and take an inventory of all your friends and activities. Which people or situations make you feel really good about yourself and which ones do not? Start eliminating the things you do that don't bolster your self-esteem. Weed your garden, so to speak! This may sound too logical, or naive, but it is astounding how many of us do things because others want us to or expect us to. Often these activities are not fulfilling at all. By being honest with ourselves, we can start recovering from codependency by doing only what feels good and uplifting to us!

A symptom one step beyond looking for love outside ourselves is to desperately seek love and approval, as pointed out in the popular country song *Achy, Breaky Heart* sung by Billy Ray Cyrus.[4] About two people breaking up, this song reflects the negativity, anger, rage and even threats of violence that can occur when people are in dysfunctional relationships based on codependency rather than love.

Achy, Breaky Heart

You can tell the world you never was my girl,
You can burn my clothes when I'm gone.
Or you can tell your friends just
what a fool I've been
and laugh and joke about me on the phone.
You can tell my arms to go back to the farm.
You can tell my feet to hit the floor.
Or you can tell my lips to tell my fingertips
they won't be reaching out for you no more.

But don't tell my heart, my achy breaky heart,
I just don't think he'd understand.
And if you tell my heart, my achy breaky heart,
he might blow up and kill this man.

This song reflects the threat that if you leave me, I might get so enraged that I would kill myself or someone else. Threats are common in dysfunctional relationships – threats of suicide or personal harm if you don't stay with me. Such threats reflect deep pain and low self-esteem such that a person would have to manipulate someone with threats to maintain a loving relationship.

Codependency and/or Caretaking

In Melody Beattie's book *Codependent No More* she describes the characteristics of codependent people:

Code*pendent people:*

> ▶ don't feel happy, content, or peaceful with themselves

> ▶ look for happiness outside themselves

> ▶ latch onto whoever or whatever they think can provide happiness

> ▶ don't love themselves

> ▶ desperately seek love and approval

> ▶ feel they *need* people more than they *want* people

> ▶ don't take time to see if other people are good for them

> ▶ don't take time to figure out if they love or like other people

> ▶ look to relationships to provide all their good feelings

All these symptoms of dependency are reflected in *Lonely Ol' Night* by John Mellencamp:[5]

Lonely Ol' Night

She calls me up and says,
"Baby, it's a lonely ol' night."
I don't know, I'm just so scared and
lonely all at the same time.
Nobody told us it was gonna work out this way.
No, no, no, no, no
I guess they knew we'd work it out in our own way.
It's a lonely ol' night.
Can I put my arms around you?
It's a lonely ol' night,
Custom made for two lonely
people like me and you.
She calls me baby. She calls everybody baby.
It's a lonely ol' night, but ain't they all?

This song reflects the desperation of some codependents. The pain from lack of self-esteem and loneliness is so intense that some people are compelled to seek sexual relationships for a quick fix. Such encounters are often accompanied by shame because they embody no real caring or love, just two people coming together out of intense emotional pain. It is like taking a drug or a drink to mask the pain.

Codependent songs often reach #1 on the pop charts. Why, you might ask. One explanation is that it is a symptom of how rampant codependency is in our society, as people like to hear music that reflects how they themselves feel. It helps affirm them as individuals and helps define their inner feelings. When we think of the power of music, it is sobering to keep the following statistics in mind: The average #1 song on the pop charts is played six to twelve times a day on the radio. This means that anyone who listens to the radio very much hears codependent lyrics quite frequently. Repetition makes these lyrics stick in the subconscious mind even more dramatically. People who additionally buy an album and listen at home get the message reinforced almost endlessly.

Another very powerful way to learn is through action or doing what is called *kinesthetic learning*. For example, when you are dancing to music, you are learning with your body. By contrast, if you read a book about the dance steps to the tango, for example, without actually performing them, you are engaging in *cerebral learning*.

Many popular songs are used in aerobics classes with the result that the messages are reinforced by the lyrics as well as kinesthetically or by the body. I took an aerobics class several years ago in which the song, *Love's Been a Little Bit Hard on Me*, was used for one of the dances. This song has a strong, driving rhythm with a very powerful repetitive beat, repeating the line "Love's been a little bit hard on me" over and over. In combina-

People like to hear music that reflects how they themselves feel. It helps affirm them as individuals and helps define their inner feelings.

tion with the negative message, the driving rhythm had the effect of going into the body as well as the subconscious mind. Whenever I hear that song, I can still feel my muscles remembering the aerobic maneuvers we did. Based on the power of kinesthetic learning, therefore, I already had a negative program in my unconscious or conscious mind about love. Dancing to that song was a way of reinforcing a negative message. It really bothered me that I could dance to the music and be in harmony with it, while at the same time leaving my body open to internalize the lyrics "Love's been a little bit hard on me." As a result, I felt I had to consciously shut that pounding message out of my mind, to affirm that love has *not* been hard on me.

The phenomenon of codependent song lyrics is not new. Many old songs also promoted this message. *I Want to Be Happy* by Vincent Youmans with lyrics by Irving Caesar is a classic song written many years ago that is still being sung.[6] The message is one of lack of boundaries; for example, I can't be happy if you are not happy. It is impossible for two individuals always to experience the same emotions. Therefore, in a relationship it is inevitable that one partner experiences an emotion which the other partner does not. Often in codependent relationships, one partner tries to manipulate the other into feeling the way he or she does. This is because such persons don't feel comfortable with their own individuality and because they have not learned proper boundaries.

I Want to Be Happy

I want to be happy
But I won't be happy,
Till I make you happy too.
Life's really worth living
When we are mirth giving,
Why can't I give some to you?

When skies are gray
And you say you are blue,
I'll send the sun smiling through.

I want to be happy
But I won't be happy,
Till I make you happy too.

No one ever talked like that to me.
I have never known such sympathy.
Only in my dreams, it really seems to me
It is too good to be true.

There are smiling faces everywhere,
Surely I deserve my little share.
I'm a lucky girl to know
That I can get it all from you.

What the words are really saying is that my boundaries are so poor that I can't have my own emotions: "If you're unhappy, I will also be unhappy" – I am powerless to have my own separate feelings from you.

Parts of this song sound very positive, such as "Life's really worth living when we are mirth giving, why can't I give some to you?" However, the tip-off that it promotes codependency is the repeated line, "I want to be happy, but, I won't be happy, till I make you happy too." What the words are really saying is that my boundaries are so poor that I can't have my own emotions: "If you're unhappy, I will also be unhappy" – I am powerless to have my own separate feelings from you.

Another line that smacks of codependency is "I'm a lucky girl to know that I can get it all from you." This is the kind of idyllic romantic love that assumes you can get all your needs met from one person. This is not true, and if you pursue this idea, you will be unfulfilled. No one will ever measure up.

Some songs help you learn about and laugh about your own dysfunction. Songwriter, singer Greg Tamblyn has written specific songs about codependency issues and recovery that are very helpful for people going through the recovery process. The following song, performed by Greg Tamblyn, *I Have A Tendency for Codependency,*[7] musically expresses some codependency issues in a tongue-and-cheek way. Perhaps by reading these lyrics you will understand these concepts at a new level.

I Have A Tendency for Codependency

I have a tendency for codependency,
And I'd sure like to make you mine.
I know we'd have it made
If you'll do things my way,
If you will only stay in line.
And live up to all my expectations
And never disappoint me at all,
We could live forever in a dream world,
So climb up on this pedestal
And baby don't you fall.

I love you, hate you, need you
I love you, hate you, need you
I love you, hate you, need you, leave me alone.

Nothing is too great a task.
Whatever is wrong with you,
I'll fix and I'll make brand new
If you'll do everything I ask.
Live up to all my expectations
Be here before I even call,
We could live forever in a dream world,
So climb up on this pedestal
And baby don't you fall.

The apparent absurdity of this song makes us laugh, yet the words are painfully true in describing many codependent relationships. There is a point in the recovery process from addictions or codependent, painful relationships where it is very healthy to laugh at ourselves. If you would like to explore more songs about recovery and addiction, see the *Sources of Sounds* section at the end of the book.

After reading this chapter and seeing different examples of songs, I hope you are wondering about your own listening habits and how they are affecting your conscious and unconscious mind. Are the songs you listen to helping you move in a positive direction or are they keeping you stuck? If you wish to change some behaviors or just gain more self-knowledge, take a serious look at the music in your environment. At the end of this chapter, the *Music Listening Diagnostic Self-Test* will help you take an overall look at your listening behavior and help evaluate its effect on your behavior.

Barbra Streisand, in her historic concert in Los Angeles after 27 years of not performing live concerts, summed up what I have been saying in this chapter. She commented:

> *One of the nice things about growing older is realizing that you can survive life's disappointments. And you also realize that you cannot look to someone else for your happiness. Of course, that screws up the songs that you can sing. You know you can't sing those dependent victim songs anymore with the same conviction. For instance, you can't sing, 'I can be happy, I can be sad, I can be good, I can be bad, it all depends on you!' Can't do that! There are songs you can sing and sing with meaning after many hours of therapy.*

The following chapter on positive song lyrics will give you some examples of what songs you can listen to after realizing that you want to recover from old dysfunctional behaviors. Any personal discoveries gleaned from the following *Music Diagnostic Self-Test* will be useful when you read about positive songs.

Music Diagnostic Self-Test

In filling out this questionnaire please be realistic and honest. For example, you might like many different kinds of music, but actually only listen to one type. Fill out the questions according to your actual behavior, not according to what you *think* you like.

When you wake up in the morning, do you turn on music to listen to?
Yes   No   (Circle one)

If "yes," what kind of music do you tend to listen to? _____

_____

_____

_____

What other times during the day are you most likely to listen to music?

_____

_____

_____

_____

Do you notice a pattern of listening to a certain type of music more at specific times of the day? For example, relaxing music at night and/or country and western music during the afternoon?

_____

_____

_____

_____

What kinds of songs with words do you prefer?

❏ Love songs   ❏ Folk songs
❏ Hymns   ❏ Country and western songs
❏ New Age songs   ❏ Protest songs
❏ Songs from musicals

Other: _____

_____

_____

_____

List titles of your current three favorite songs.

1. _____

2. _____

3. _____

Having thought about and listed your songs, do you see a pattern to the lyrics you are most drawn to?   Yes   No   (Circle one)

If "yes," explain the pattern:

_____

_____

_____

_____

_____

_____

_____

_____

Music without words – which type do you listen to the most?

- ❏ Classical - orchestral
- ❏ Baroque
- ❏ Gregorian chants
- ❏ Blues
- ❏ Easy listening
- ❏ Drumming
- ❏ Rock & roll
- ❏ Ragtime
- ❏ Chamber music
- ❏ Renaissance
- ❏ 20th century classical music
- ❏ New Age
- ❏ Elevator music
- ❏ Jazz
- ❏ Heavy metal rock

Of these choices, music without words, which if any of them do you find repulsive? _____

_____

_____

_____

_____

_____

Explain why? _____

_____

_____

_____

_____

_____

_____

_____

_____

How would you describe the music you are most drawn to? Check all that apply:

❏ Fast-paced   ❏ Slow
❏ Syncopated   ❏ Sad
❏ Melancholy   ❏ Uplifting
❏ Joyful   ❏ Spiritual
❏ Hard driving rhythms   ❏ Romantic
❏ Angry   ❏ Relaxing

Other: _____

_____

_____

_____

Have you at one time in your life had a favorite singer and now realize that you no longer enjoy this artist?   Yes   No   (Circle one)

If "yes," who is the singer? _____

_____

_____

Explain why you feel you have lost interest in that particular musical artist: _____

_____

_____

_____

_____

_____

_____

Which instruments do you currently find the most pleasant for listening? Check all that apply:

❏ Strings, in general   ❏ Piano
❏ Violin   ❏ Cello
❏ Acoustic guitar   ❏ Electric guitar
❏ Brass instruments   ❏ Percussion
❏ Flute   ❏ Clarinet
❏ Saxophone   ❏ Accordion
❏ Harp   ❏ Organ

Are any of the above instruments hard for you to listen to or even painful to your ear?   Yes   No   (Circle one)

If "yes," please list: _____

_____

_____

_____

_____

_____

Thinking back over your life and musical experiences, do you see any big changes in your taste in music or patterns to your musical listening behavior, such as loving organ music in your 20s and never listening to it in your 40s. Thinking of decades of your life, are there patterns to your musical taste?   Yes   No   (Circle one)

If "yes," please describe:

In your 20s: _____

_____

_____

_____

In your 30s: _____

_____

_____

_____

In your 40s: _____

_____

_____

_____

In your 50s: _____

_____

_____

_____

In your 60s: _____

_____

_____

_____

In your 70s: _____

_____

_____

_____

Did you enjoy filling out this survey?
     Yes   No   Neutral   (Circle one)

Please explain: _____

_____

_____

_____

_____

_____

_____

Did you learn anything new about your musical listening habits as a result of filling this form out?   Yes   No   (Circle one)

If "yes," please explain: _____

_____

_____

_____

_____

_____

_____

_____

Evaluation of Music Diagnostic Self-Test

Just like art, music can be used as a projective technique. I have noticed over the years that there are patterns to what music people really like and what music they really dislike or are even repulsed by. For example, individuals who are diagnosed as depressed prefer blues to happy, uplifting music. Quite a few scientific studies document this clinical observation, yet it is not something that people are usually conscious of. The process of being drawn to music or some art form is unconscious, reflecting inner reality.

Thus, the music we are drawn to reveals a lot about what is going on inside of us at any given moment. In this way music could be compared to the Rohrschah inkblot tests and can be used as a projective psychological test. For example, when you look at an inkblot test and you project anger into every inkblot, it is obvious that you have anger issues bubbling inside of you. There are inkblots that are more obvious than others, for example, butterflies. People who see something other than butterflies have more of a creative streak.

Music for Mellow Minds is a relaxation tape that I wrote in a minor key. Minor keys are usually considered more sad than major keys. And yet, when people are in a deep state of relaxation, I have found a minor key doesn't feel sad unless the person is experiencing sadness within. I have taken thousands of people through deep relaxation sessions with this music in a minor key, and most people report happy feelings, serene feelings and often visualize themselves dancing joyfully to the music.

I have found that people who are feeling powerless in some way have an adverse reaction to vocal music that has powerful strong voices. For example, *Beethoven's 9th Symphony, the 4th movement*, includes very strong vocal parts and a quartet with voices interweaving at one point. Some people are angered by these strong voices. Women who are feeling powerless will usually say they don't like the voices in the music. This is symbolic of their rejection of their own feminine powers, especially the power of self-expression. Men who are angry at their dominant mothers or wives do not like the strong female voices either.

One tape that has had dramatic results this way is Susan Osborne's tape, *Susan*. One side has an improvisation of *Amazing Grace*. Most individuals do not recognize it as that old tune, but hear her powerful voice. I have used this tape with hundreds of clients in sessions, and reactions are very seldom neutral. People are either very positive and identify with her self-expressive power or they feel anger at her and perceive her as shouting and being too dominant.

What Do Your Musical Tastes Imply?

If you find a pattern of listening only to very loud, fast-paced music all day, you are probably highly stressed, are most likely an A-type personality and may be addicted to loud chaotic sound. If you feel a change of music would at least partially be positive, refer to some of the relaxation music listed in this book and try consciously changing some of your music listening habits and see if it affects any part of your life that you would like to change.

If you listen to country and western and/or blues all day, you may be depressed. Research shows that if this is all you find yourself listening to, it probably reflects a sense of depression and the music is affirming your internal emotional state.

If you wake up and listen to fast music to help awaken you and you choose other kinds of music for other reasons during the day, then you are using music in a healthy manner.

If you find yourself listening to romantic songs with codependent lyrics repeatedly, take a look at your life and see how this reflects what is going on with you. Are your relationships healthy? Are the songs reflecting any patterns that you would like to change?

Instruments That You Are Drawn to:

Flute – Flutes usually reflect happy feelings and help your imagination be free. They tend to take you out of the body and into the realm of the imagination and facilitate floating feelings.

Strings – If you are especially drawn to violins, cellos and violas, you may need grounding. Violins are romantic and a combination string effect can create a grounded, safe feeling. Strings are usually played rather legato or smoothly, which also creates a safe, soothing feeling.

Piano – Pianos are more earthy than flutes. They also can create a grounded feeling and keep you down to earth.

Percussion – Percussion can help bring up anger or can be used for getting into an altered state if the beat is steady.

Brass – Brass can be good for increasing feelings of power and increasing energy level.

Organ – The organ is also a power instrument. It can be good for facilitating feelings of inner power. Some people have hangups about the organ because they associate it with church and childhood religious experiences that they found unpleasant or didn't agree with.

Most people don't take the time to thoroughly analyze their music listening habits. The *Music Diagnostic Self-Test* helps you to see patterns in your listening and how they may effect your life and emotions in other areas. Now that you have completed the test, the next chapter on positive songs will help you further understand how the music in your life can be a tool for transformation.

6

POSITIVE SONGS – SONGS FOR RECOVERY

Barbra Streisand's comments at the end of the previous chapter expressed a dislike of "dependent victim songs" and underscored that she could no longer sing such songs with conviction. However, she emphasized that there are positive, healthy songs like one of her favorites, *On a Clear Day*.[1] Read the lyrics for yourself and see how you would rate this song in terms of positive lyrics.

On a Clear Day

On a clear day, rise and look around you,
And you'll see who you are.
On a clear day, how it will astound you,
That the glow of your being outshines ev'ry star.
You feel part of ev'ry mountain, sea and shore.
You can hear, from far and near,
a world you've never heard before.
And on a clear day, on that clear day,
You can see forever and ever more.

If my theory is true that negative song lyrics can perpetuate and promote codependency, then the opposite must also be true. That is, songs with positive lyrics can strengthen our inner lives and motivate us to behave more positively. Based on this conviction, I challenge the mass-market song writers to compose more self-empowering lyrics.

Another Streisand song, *The Way He Makes Me Feel*,[2] is positive because it is about a woman's awareness of how she is feeling. It reveals her inner struggle to understand different or unsettling feelings.

The Way He Makes Me Feel

There's no chill
and yet I shiver.
There's no flame
and yet I burn.
I'm not sure what I'm afraid of
and yet I'm trembling.

There's no storm
but I hear thunder
and I'm breathless,
why, I wonder.
Weak, one moment,
then the next I'm fine.

I feel as if I'm falling every time I close my eyes,
and flowing through my body is a river of surprise.
Feelings are awakening I hardly recognize as mine.
What are all these new sensations?
What's the secret they reveal?
I'm not sure I understand, but I like the way I feel.

Why is it every time I close my eyes, he's there?
The water shining on his skin
the sunlight in his hair.
All the while I am thinking of things
that I can share with him.
I'm a bundle of confusion.
Yet it has a strange appeal.
Did it all begin with him
and the way he makes me feel?
I like the way he makes me feel.

One could argue that the "falling in love" in this song might refer to codependent feelings. However, at least the song describes an experience that is both emotional and very physical, "flowing through my body is a river of surprise." The song discusses the person's feelings and experiences as opposed to being "other-oriented." For example, the first stanza, "There's no chill and yet I shiver. There's no flame and yet I burn," seems an honest attempt at describing feelings and trying to understand where they are coming from and what they mean.

Feelings always have a message. Sometimes it is difficult to translate feelings into meaningful thoughts that we can verbalize, however, we must strive to express and communicate our feelings in order that they can be acknowledged and dealt with. Jumbled, confused feelings can sabotage our careers and relationships. For example, have you ever been upset by a conversation with someone without knowing why you were upset? After staying with the feeling and thinking about it, the real answer usually comes to us. That awareness is always a good feeling because it clears confusion.

I use these ideas in my therapy. If someone comes to me saying, "I feel bad about my husband and I don't know why," or if someone reports unexplained upsetting, or anxious feelings, I use music to help them get more in touch with their feelings. The client can then translate, and hopefully understand, the core of his or her unclear discomfort. Sometimes the words of songs or the words and the music together can help us identify and clarify what our feelings are trying to tell us.

Song Lyrics and Positive Affirmations – Are They Related?

Many books have been written about positive affirmations, that is repetitious written or verbal positive sayings in the present tense. Present tense is important because it indicates to the subconscious that you are healed or prosperous (or whatever condition you want to change) right now. If you indicated that you will be something more positive in the future, then that gives the subconscious a message that you feel lesser about yourself right now. Some teachers suggest that you stand in front of a mirror and repeat positive affirmations at least 100 times several times a day. For example, you could repeat, "I am prosperity," or "I am love," etc., hundreds of times in an effort to bring about these positive states or behaviors. The theory is that repeating "I am love" or "I am prosperity" sends your subconscious a positive message, intended to change a negative thought to a positive thought and eventually changing your outer behavior. It is important to always affirm what you do want, not want you don't want.

One of the reasons that affirmations work is that everything is created in our mental plane before it can become a reality. But if you are experiencing panic attacks and are feeling very fearful and vulnerable, you may feel silly saying the following affirmation: "I am safe." You may think, but this is not the truth – my heart is pounding from fear and I feel vulnerable from my head down to my toes. It may seem stupid or even hypocritical to affirm the opposite of what you are feeling. Your words are powerful, however, and once you start affirming that you are safe, a change starts to take place. You may not feel it, but it is important to continue the affirmations so that you change your subconscious mind-set, which creates your physical reality.

I personally believe in the idea of giving positive affirmations to the subconscious and have seen it work. However, in our busy lives, it is difficult for many of us to be so disciplined that we can stop everything several times a day to perform positive affirmations. An alternative way of getting positive affirmations is to listen to music with positive lyrics because these ideas also sink into your subconscious. This particularly works well if you listen with the idea of allowing the words and music to enter your body and psyche. Listening with this kind of conscious receptivity helps you take in the positive message at a deeper level.

Some of the new consciousness songs that are being written contain very positive messages and can be used as positive affirmations of your inner wisdom. For example, the song *It's in Every One of Us*[3] sends the message that we all have inner wisdom and that by waking up and realizing our own power, we can create a better reality.

It's in Every One of Us

It's in every one of us
To be wise.
Find your heart and open up both your eyes.
We can all know everything
Without ever knowing why.
It's in every one of us
By and by.

It's in every one of us.
I just remembered.
It's like I've been sleeping for years,
Not awake as I could be.
But my seeing is better
And I can see, through the tears.

And I've been realizing that I bought this ticket,
But I've been watching only half of the show.
And there is scenery and lights,
And a cast of thousands who all know
What I know.
And it's good that it is so.

Why Use Musical Affirmations over Spoken Affirmations?

Hearing songs and thinking of the words as a positive affirmation for yourself is less inhibitiing than speaking them in front of a mirror.

You might wonder why bother with musical affirmations when you can just speak the words or think the thoughts? There are several reasons. One reason is that many individuals feel too inhibited to stand in front of their mirrors and speak affirmations and, therefore, they just don't choose this option for personal growth or changing a behavior. Another reason is that the rhythm of music can help to drive the thought into your subconscious. I mentioned the aerobics class in a previous chapter and how the driving rhythm of a song helped ingrain the words in my mind and body, whether I wanted it to or not. Hearing songs and thinking of the words as a positive affirmation for yourself is less inhibiting than speaking them in front of a mirror. It can be a good place to start the process. Another reason is that music speaks to your emotional self. If you just say the words with no feeling, the results are not as beneficial as when you feel the words in addition to intellectualizing them. Music helps integrate your intellect with your feeling self, and integrating these two are necessary for changing negative behaviors.

Using the idea that songs can be our affirmations, it is important to analyze which songs are good for which situations. The following songs address the idea of overcoming difficult situations and can be very helpful in building up your inner resources.

Songs about Overcoming

Dr. Gordon Hodas, a child and family psychiatrist, is committed to the concept of music and healing. He has demonstrated this committment by composing special songs that focus on the theme that struggle can lead to positive outcomes. One of his songs, for example, *Stretch Yourself,* is about taking emotional risks and being able to express both negative and positive feelings. (see Sources of Sounds in appendix)

Stretch Yourself!

You want to make a friend
But you're much too shy
Stretch yourself!

You're feeling so lonely
You're about to cry
Stretch yourself!

Taking a chance
You stand to win
If you just lie down
You'll never begin
You're a fish out of water
But you know how to swim
Stretch yourself!

You want to say, I love you
But you don't know how
Stretch yourself!

You're feeling real angry
But you don't want a row
Stretch yourself!

You can say what you mean
And with practice, get good
Feel much better

When you're understood
Your self-respect
Will grow like it should
Stretch yourself!

Muscles when they're stretched
They hurt and ache
Stretch yourself!

At first you might think
You made a mistake
Stretch yourself!

But after a while
Your body's not sore
You move all around
More than before
Your confidence grows
More and more
Stretch yourself!

Another powerful song by Dr. Hodas is *Thinkin about my Poppa*, an emotionally gripping song about a father who was emotionally absent. The song helps the listener cope with the phantom feelings that come with a father *who is there but isn't there*, and also helps the listener grieve the loss and then move on to be a better parent than the previous generation. Dr. Hodas comments:

I believe that, in addition to promoting problem-solving, the use of music can highlight the spiritual dimension of psychotherapy. This dimension is critical because therapy succeeds, I believe, when it creates a context that clarifies and even transforms an individual's or family's sense of meaning.

As an individual reader you can determine which exercises in this book fit in your comfort zone and do these musical exercises in the privacy of your own home. However, some therapists want to incorporate music in their work and have fears of appearing unprofessional or awkward as they try some of these new techniques. Dr. Hodas has valuable thoughts on this subject:

> *Such concerns, I believe, are often a curse of graduate and medical schools: making helpers so self-conscious that creative instincts are suppressed. To be sure, professional boundaries are essential, but too often such boundaries become so narrow that psychotherapy becomes sterile.*

We have been discussing songs written specifically for overcoming, however, there are many popular songs that were not written for a therapeutic purpose that can have a positive message. For example, *Gonna Build a Mountain*[4] "from the musical production *Stop the World - I Want to Get Off* is a very positive song about overcoming a negative situation. If you know the tune, sing along in your mind as you read the words. Notice that the rhythm and melodic line convey a very hopeful feeling. The rhythm moves in a convincing way that helps create a feeling of "Yes, I can do it!"

Gonna Build a Mountain

Gon-na build a mountain, from a little hill.
Gon-na build a mountain, least I hope I will.
Gon-na build a mountain, gonna build it high.
I don't know how I'm gonna do it
Only know I'm gonna try.

Gon-na build a daydream, from a little hope.
Gon-na push that daydream, up the mountain slope.

Gon-na build a daydream, gonna see it through.
Gon-na build a mountain and a daydream
Gon-na make em both come true.

Gon-na build a heaven from a little hell.
Gon-na build a heaven and I know darn well.
If I build my mountain with a lot of care.
And take my daydream up the mountain,
Heaven will be waiting there.

Another positive song about building a dream is *Climb Every Mountain*[5] from *The Sound of Music*. Think of the music as you read the words and notice the difference between this and *Gonna Build a Mountain*. In *Climb Every Mountain*, the music brings about a more quiet, powerful feeling, which gradually makes the listener feel a sort of reverence for something higher, of a spiritual nature.

Climb Every Mountain

Climb ev-ry mountain, search high and low,
Follow ev-ry by-way, ev-ry path you know.
Climb ev-ry mountain, ford every stream,
Follow ev-ry rainbow, till you find your dream.

A dream that will need, all the love you can give,
Ev-ry day of your life for as long as you live.
Climb ev-ry mountain, ford ev-ry stream,
Follow ev-ry rainbow, till you find your dream!

If you are building something or have a dream that you want to manifest, listen to these songs often, sing them, and try hard to identify with the lyrics on a feeling level. Feel the building or action energy start to grow within your body. These songs will help you identify with your goal and help build your inner resources. If you say you have a dream but simultaneously feel empty inside, it is extremely difficult for your dream/goal to manifest itself. However, if you keep building your inner feeling about it, you cannot fail.

Why Is It Important to Sing the Songs?

Singing affirmations has stronger therapeutic power than just speaking the words.

Listening to the songs can serve as your positive affirmations; however, *singing* the songs at the same time is much more effective because singing makes you breathe deeply. Breathing is very important for bringing about change in the body and mind. This is why breathing is so important in the practice of yoga, for example. Singing high tones creates resonance in the head and is more difficult than singing low tones which creates resonance in the chest and abdomen. While the act of singing forces you to breathe more deeply, the resonance forces movement inside the body, which can help stale energy move out and be replaced by more vital energy. This is why people often feel so invigorated by singing – it is actually a physiological happening in the body as well as possibly creating an emotional change. Singing affirmations has stronger therapeutic power than just speaking the words. Dr. Diamond has confirmed this fact with his kinesiology tests, i.e., muscle testing shows stronger muscular strength after *singing* words than just *speaking* the same words.[6]

I envision a day when people will get together with friends and sing songs that reflect their goals. Imagine the power of such a group. Already, people get together for self-help in 12-step groups, all kinds of support groups, mastermind and meditation groups. What about singing affirmation groups? Perhaps you could start one and witness how empowering it can be.

Songs for Recovery

Musician Greg Tamblyn's song, *Unconditional Love (The Story of Evy),*[7] is a true story about a woman who had Lou Gehrig's disease. She was gradually deteriorating and was only given six months to live. This very powerful song tells the story of her illness and her journey of healing.

Unconditional Love (The Story of Evy)

Evy had a body like a bowl of jelly in a wheelchair.
Evy had a nerve disease   all she
could do was sit there.
Evy was wasting away, her muscles all in decay.
She heard the doctor say, "Six months to live."

Evy always said she hated her body,
she was overweight.
And now a disease was making her thin -
What a twist of fate.

She was almost out of time,
But somewhere in her mind -
There was something in her mind
She had to find out if she could get.

Chorus: She said, "It's something
called unconditional love.
Supposed to be really wonderful stuff.
I've heard if you can get enough,
you can find peace.
So in the time that I've got left
I got to find some for myself.
I believe unconditional love is what I need."

Since all Evy could do is sit in a wheelchair
Evy rolled it over and sat there in front of the mirror.
She looked at her body and recalled
every negative thought,
And though there were a lot,
she wrote them all down.

Now every day Evy would sit there naked
at the mirror and look,
Till she found one good thing about herself
to write in her book.
And after a few months time
Her thoughts began to grow kind.
And the negative words in her mind
Could not be found.

But a funny thing happened when Evy started
Learning to love herself.
The deterioration just stopped,
then reversed itself.
Evy was moving her arms and legs
and starting to feel.
Yes, a funny thing happened,
Evy started to heal.

She said, "It feels like unconditional love
And it's really wonderful stuff.
I've heard if you can get enough,
you can find peace.
So in the time that you've got left
You better find some for yourself.
I believe unconditional love is what we all need."

Healing must start in the mind. Evy is alive and well today – a living example that, no matter how serious one's problem or illness, we can replace negative thoughts with loving thoughts and start the healing process.

This true story illustrates how healing must start in the mind. Evy is alive and well today – a living example that, no matter how serious one's problem or illness, we can replace negative thoughts with loving thoughts and start the healing process. It is never too late to start stripping away the old negatives and replacing them with loving affirmations. The power of positive, loving thoughts or affirmations is astounding. Anyone who has sent negative messages to their body could benefit from this uplifting story in the form of song. Every time I hear this song, I feel unconditional love and am reminded of how important it is to remember this lesson.

In another song about recovery, *You Can't Blame the Wreck on the Train*,[8] Greg Tamblyn sings about recovery from negative, addictive relationships. This song is a reminder of the need to move on from old destructive, codependent behaviors. Often hittng our humor buttons, the song underscores the importance of not blaming others, but, instead, taking responsibility for our own actions.

You Can't Blame the Wreck on the Train

I got crazy yesterday and I called her to say,
Baby, please, won't you come home tonight?
I can't even trust my brain
To get my heart in from the rain.

She's a hurricane alright.

Early this morning after she was gone,
I sat there in a chair all alone.
Called my best friend crying -
Asking him why she always treats me wrong.

How many times have I promised myself
Not to do the same things as before.
I swear I'll leave it alone and believe it
Then turn around and do it some more.

Fool me once and its shame on you,
Fool me twice and its shame on me.
There was my best friends warning
When I called him this morning.

He said, "When the gates are all down
And the signals are flashing
and the whistle is screaming in vain,
And you stay on the tracks, ignoring the facts,
Well, you can't blame the wreck on the train.
No, you can't blame the train.
Man, you gotta quit blaming that train."

This song addresses the issue of taking responsibility for our actions and admitting that we create our own reality. By doing this, we reject the codependent habit of being the poor-me victim. Recovery from addictions, bad relationships, or any other problem behavior means taking responsibility for our actions and, metaphorically speaking, quit blaming the wreck on the train.

Another story of recovery with the help of a song was shared by a minister one Sunday morning at a well-known Unity Church. The minister told of her recovery from addiction to alcohol. It was a very touching story that particularly struck me, because she spoke about how she used songs as positive affirmations to facilitate her recovery. She mentioned the song, Let Me Remember,[9] which is about raising our consciousness and realizing that we have a higher power that is really in control. Listening to this song over and over, she used its words as a positive affirmation and could feel it changing her at the cellular level.

Let Me Remember

Into His Prescence
Would I enter now.
For I am surrounded
By the love of God.

Let me be still
And listen to the truth.
Let every voice
But God's be still in me.

Let me remember
I am one with God.
Peace to my brother
Who is one with me.

Let me remember
What my purpose is.
Let all the world
Be blessed with peace through me.

There is one light
And that I share with Him.
I am sustained by the love of God.
All that I give is given to myself.

Let me remember
There is no will but God's.
His peace is with me.
Forever I am safe.

Let me remember
There is no love but God's.
I will step back
And let Him lead the way.

This song would be good to listen to if you are interested in spiritual surrender. Also, if you are searching for a purpose in your life and/or work, listen to this song many times. It will constantly remind you and your higher self that you are serious about surrendering to a higher power.

Songs about Grief and Loss

Ken Medema, a music therapist who happens to be blind, has an extraordinary talent for creating songs for specific feelings and situations. In his three-tape album *Where Do I Go from Here? A Musical Dialogue in the Journey of Loss and Grief*, he sings songs about difficult aspects of the grieving process that relate to very specific aspects of a person's life; for example, one of the songs deals with the death of his childhood dog. Another song, *Gotta Find a Better Way*,[10] particularly impacted me.

Gotta Find a Better Way

When it seems I am always running,
Running from a private nightmare,
I can't tell anybody.
They have got problems of their own.

And when I think that I have escaped it,
Its there behind me.
And I'm stumbling as I'm running
through this long and lonely night.
I once believed in morning
But I will not see that light.
And I wonder if there will ever be a time
when I will ever be all right.
I only want to be all right.

Can't you see me reaching out,
Reachin for a new direction.
And every time I think I've found it,
It blows up in my hand.
And I've tried everything I know of
And it all goes down in ashes.
And I know there must be something
To help me with this pain.

A bridge I can walk on
That won't give me needless strain.
Somebody who's gonna hold me close
And tell me I can be OK again.

There's got to be a better way.
There's got to be a better dream.
Won't somebody please come tell me
Life is not as bad as it may seem.
Where all my plans have crashed and burned
And there is nothing more to say,
I won't go on unless I know
I can find a better way.
Gotta find that better way.
Gotta dream a better way.

I don't trust people talkin,
You know their words come down so easily.
When you really need somebody
They turn and run away – yeah.
Oh, I am left alone as always
No way to face tomorrow.
No, there must be someone
Who will dare to know me well.
Somebody who is going to listen
When I have got so much to tell.
Somebody who will help me find
A way to get beyond this living hell.

The music can help you feel more authentic.

This Ken Medema song is particularly important because it captures that lonely, isolated feeling one can experience if going through the loss of a loved one, depression, panic attacks, etc. – any difficult personal feeling that is not generally shared by those surrounding us. For example, when Ken sings, "I don't trust people talkin, you know their words come down so easily," it reminds me of empty words some people use in response to a friend hurting. Often simple solutions are offered which lack compassion for the depth of the other person's feeling, for example, "everything will be alright." Therefore, for those experiencing a "dark night of the soul," isolated from friends and family who are not able to or don't want to deal with someone else's emotional pain, the words, "there must be someone who will dare to know me well," must sound very familiar, true and hopeful.

If you are going through a difficult time of grief or loss, listen to music that helps you feel more deeply, and that helps you get down to the soul level where healing takes place. The music can help you feel more authentic. Don't be afraid to grieve and feel deeply. Just remember that even if it is painful, it is much better to feel intensely than to be numb to life.

We have been discussing songs that fit a particular niche, like recovery, grief, or overcoming. This is working in a framework of a large concept or type of song. However, in the next section, instead of discussing songs for affirmations, we are going to discuss songs that match your mood in a particular moment. This is related to something called the *iso principle*. In music therapy work there is a theory that to help a patient change you must use the iso principle or in other words, you must match the mood of the music to the mood of the patient before you can move them into another state of mind. This is not always true, because in some cases, you can instantly change someone's mood by using the opposite music. However, the iso principle can be a very powerful tool for therapy. The next section will give you tools to explore this idea in your own personal exploration.

Songs That Match Your Mood

Exploring feelings can be exhilarating and also very frustrating. Sometimes feelings are so intense and painful that we just want to shut them out in any way we can. People do this by numbing themselves with workaholism, food, alcohol, drugs, etc. Depressing feelings, for example, can be so painful that we just want to take a pill and make them go away. However, exploring our feelings in a natural way can be very rewarding. Trusting the psyche to lead us beyond painful barriers is important in this process.

One way to explore feelings is to search for songs that reflect our feelings. This may sound overly simple at first, but after you begin the process, you will be surprised at what you learn about your feelings. For example, one of my clients, Kate, suffered from panic attacks. Kate wanted to go deeper into her feelings while in a panic so she could find the source of the panic.

If you are grieving and find a song about grief, for example, it can make you feel affirmed to know that someone felt as badly as you do and that he or she took the time to write a song about it.

However, rational thinking is extremely difficult while you are in a panic attack, so she was not very successful. Instead, I had her explore her feelings and search for songs that reflected her feelings while in the middle of an attack. Specifically, I gave Kate a big stack of song books and told her to find five songs that matched her feelings.

I explained to Kate that there is tremendous power in songs that reflect how you feel. As mentioned, research has documented that depressed people prefer depressing music such as the blues or country and western songs about victims or poor me songs. It is not therapeutic to reinforce your own negative feelings by listening to negative songs over and over; however, it is positive and helpful to find a song that reflects how you feel. If you are grieving and find a song about grief, for example, it can make you feel affirmed to know that someone felt as badly as you do and that he or she took the time to write a song about it.

Kate shared with me her initial skepticism toward this exercise, stating that it seemed almost trite; however, she was thrilled at the end because the process of finding songs that matched her feelings helped her define some of her issues. Out of the five songs she chose, the one that meant the most to her was *The Music of the Night*[11] from the popular musical, *The Phantom of the Opera*.

The Music of the Night

Night time sharpens, heightens each sensation,
Darkness stirs and wakes imagination.
Silently the senses abandon their defenses.

Slowly, gently, night unfolds its splendor,
Grasp it, sense it, tremulous and tender.
Turn your face away from the garish light of day,
Turn your thoughts away from cold unfeeling light,
And listen to the music of the night.

Close your eyes and surrender
to your darkest dreams.
Purge your thoughts of the life you knew before.
Close your eyes, let your spirit start to soar,
And you'll live as you've never lived before.

Slowly, deftly, music shall caress you,
Hear it, feel it, secretly possess you.
Open up your mind, let your fantasies unwind,
In the darkness which you know you cannot fight.
The darkness of the music of the night.

Let your mind start a journey through
a strange new world.
Release all thoughts of the world
you knew before.
Let your soul take you where you long to be,
Only then can you belong to me.

Floating, falling, sweet intoxication,
Touch me, trust me, savor each sensation.
Let the dream begin, let your darker side give in,
To the power of the music that I write.
The power of the music of the night.

You alone can make my song take flight.
Help me make the music of the night.

Along with her panic attacks, Kate also had become fearful of being alone at night, whereas previously she had never experienced any fear at night. This song helped her see that the fear of the dark was like the fear of her feelings: Feelings can seem dark and mysterious. The song talks about "darkness stirring the imagination" and uses the metaphors of night and day to contrast the difference between imagination, deep feeling and music to "cold unfeeling light."

The words "surrender to your darkest dreams" meant to Kate that she needed to surrender to her fears and deep, dark feelings. When she read the line, "slowly, deftly, music shall caress you, hear it, feel it, secretly possess you," Kate decided to allow her feelings to start caressing her and possessing her in the sense of honoring them rather than trying to shut them out. As a result, she made a conscious decision to allow her feelings to guide her down her path of personal growth where she longed to be. Kate is a creative person, already aware of many of her feelings; however, the following song exercise helped her go deeper into the feeling level and start the process of overcoming her panic attacks.

Exercise: Match a Feeling to a Song

Write a goal or problem that you are working on in the space below. List songs that match your feelings about this issue/situation. Most of us do not have great memories about song lyrics, so to help you in this process, you may want to look through song books or cassette or album covers to help spur your memory. Before starting the exercise, it is best to assemble several song books so you have plenty of songs to choose from. Start by choosing 5 to 7 songs that match your feelings. Write these songs down and then carefully reread the lyrics to get a feeling of how each song relates to your present issue.

Goal or problem: _____

_____

_____

_____

_____

_____

_____

List of songs that match the above feeling:

1. _____

2. _____

3, _____

4. _____

5. _____

6. _____

7. _____

Positive Song Exercise

If you want to try using songs as affirmations, make a list of positive songs you know. They can include songs that you know from memory, or that you have on tapes, compact discs, or sheet music. Determine which songs could be positive affirmations for you. You may put them in the following categories:

Songs for Recovery: _____

_____

_____

_____

_____

_____

_____

Songs for Overcoming: _____

_____

_____

_____

_____

Songs to Build Inner Wisdom: _____

_____

_____

_____

_____

Songs for Spiritual Growth: _____

_____

_____

_____

_____

Songs for Humor: _____

_____

_____

_____

_____

Make a commitment to the number of times you will listen to particular songs every day or week until you feel they have sufficiently incorporated their essence into your subconscious.

After you have made your list, make a commitment to the number of times you will listen to particular songs every day or week until you feel they have sufficiently incorporated their essence into your subconscious. You will know this has happened when you feel you have learned the lesson from the song. For example, I had a client who dreamt of starting her own business. She talked about it for years, but always manufactured reasons why she could not move ahead and actually do it. She was all words and no action. This became more and more frustrating with each passing year. One day the realization hit her that she was afraid to follow her dream, so she tried using songs as affirmations. Every morning she listened to a recording of *Climb Every Mountain* and tried to identify with the words. At first she could just listen, then she started to sing the words along with the recording, which made them seem even more real. Finally, she found herself taking the necessary steps to follow her dream by starting her business.

Hopefully, some of the techniques offered in this chapter will open new windows for personal growth. Songs are a resource that most individuals have easy access to through sources such as libraries, radio, song books, etc. Finding the deeper meaning to our feelings through songs can be an exciting inner journey, one that can be solitary or shared by others. Enjoy your journey!

CHAPTER 7

INNER POWER THROUGH MUSIC

In previous chapters we unearthed childhood issues and worked on body awareness. Now it is time to tie all these areas together by building inner power. In his book, *The Celestine Prophecy,* author James Redfield talks about meditating in scenic places in nature and concentrating on drawing the energy from the beauty that surrounds us into our own being.

This chapter will show how you can apply this idea to music. Extracting beauty from nature is easier when done with music. As you will understand after practicing the exercises at the end of this chapter, the right kind of music provides energy and power that help you draw extra power into your being. But the key is choosing the right music and knowing how to direct your thoughts as you listen.

After experiencing these exercises, most people report a significant increase in feelings of inner power. Many find power over food and other addictions. Others report a stronger sense of well-being and inner peace.

This chapter is based on a series of classes on Inner Power Through Music I have taught over a 10-year period. In these classes, we discuss different kinds of power. Then, while the participants lie on mats on the floor, I take them through different kinds of inner power exercises verbally, fol-

To the eye appeals the outer man, the inner to the ear.

– Wagner

The right kind of music provides energy and power that help you draw extra power into your being.

lowed by the appropriate music. Similarly, in this chapter, different kinds of inner power will be discussed, the exercises will be introduced and the recommended music will be listed, so you can work on your inner power through music at home. Several choices of music will be suggested for each kind of inner power, so you can experiment with what works best for you.

To understand inner power, we must explore the concept of inner *and* outer or external power. External power and inner power are closely connected. Inner power builds up in us as a result of both inner and outer experiences. Some of the external power experiences that help build inner power includes success in music, art, sports, relationships and accomplishing tasks that are important to us. To a small toddler who has never left her mother's side, just walking to the basement of her house on her own, is an example of outer power that builds inner power. This one experience leads to the self-confidence to explore other rooms without the security of the mother's presence. This process of outer power building our internal power continues throughout our lives.

There are people in the public eye who have outer power experiences all the time but do not necessarily translate to inner power. For example, Barbara Streisand, singer extraordinaire, adored by millions, developed a phobia of singing in public, despite this adoration. We all need a balance between external power experiences and inner power experiences.

Some kinds of inner experiences have very little to do with external power. For example, I was once in the basement of a library looking up a periodical for a research study. Recently I had been focusing on a phobia that I wanted to resolve and out of the clear blue, I heard a tiny voice in my head say, "If you are really willing to let go of this problem, you will feel a spiritual presence and be able to let go of it." It was a powerful "let go, let God" experience, which seemingly had nothing to do with my being in the basement of a library. In other words, I would put this in the category of an inner power experience.

In some of the inner power exercises in this chapter, you will have an opportunity to experience forms of power on the inner plane that would be impossible to experience in real life. Think of the kind of power Princess Diana must feel when she is in public and receives adoration from thousands of people. Or the kind of power Luciano Pavaratti must feel when he walks out to sing to thousands of people. Even though the majority of us will never experience this kind of power, you can experience something very similar on the inner plane with music.

Ideally, as children we should feel power through accomplishment and love from our parents. If you identified areas where you lack in personal power after reading the inner child chapter, this is the chapter that will help you work on and build up inner power resources. Think of building inner power like building muscles. You don't have to go to a gym to do it, you can do the exercises in your own home, alone, or with friends.

We will be working with seven different kinds of power:

- ▶ Quiet inner power
- ▶ Spiritual power
- ▶ Energized power
- ▶ Physical power
- ▶ Power from risk taking
- ▶ Power from love
- ▶ Power over food

As the seven kinds of power are described, ask yourself which ones come naturally to you and which ones would be beneficial to cultivate as a way to enhance your life.

Quiet Inner Power

Quiet inner power is best described as the kind of power you can experience from a walk in nature – from a beautiful forest, lake or ocean. A good example of this kind of power is the feeling of serenity and power one gets from a sailboat ride – feeling the wind in your face and being in harmony with the wind and water. It is the sense of quiet – hearing sounds and taking in the sweet smell of fresh water and foliage versus motor sounds and the smell of gasoline. Quiet inner power can also come from very simple experiences in your own home such as watching squirrels playing and feeling a sense of joy and harmony with nature.

There's music in the sighing of a reed,
There's music in the gushing of a rill,
There's music in all things, if men had ears.
The earth is but an echo of the spheres.
– Lord Byron

Another kind of quiet inner power comes from being very focused on a project, perhaps quilting, woodworking or painting and feeling totally absorbed and fulfilled from the process. This is similar to what happens in meditation – where we focus our minds completely on one thing or one thought. If you have experienced this kind of focus, you know the sense of inner power it brings. Occasionally, while writing this book I have become completely absorbed and forgot about time, place, hunger, etc.

Spiritual Power

Spiritual power is similar to quiet inner power, except that it also brings a clear feeling of connection with a higher power. This connection can be a sensation or an actual vision of white light. Many people report seeing Jesus, angels or other beings they sense are from a spiritual realm. Spiritual power can be either very inner and quiet or quite dramatic! For example, the following is an experience that spontaneously occurred in an inner power session:

It feels like the earth has become a womb and I am an embryo

I see a stone which is becoming an egg. Inside is the white and yolk. The eyes have turned inward and they see the yolk pulsating like a heartbeat. Fairly rapidly. The yolk becomes bright red. There is a sense of power about it. Almost a feeling of fear that something is about to happen. The yolk fills up the whole egg. The egg cracks and the yolk spills out like blood. It frightens me a little. Now the yolk is being absorbed into the ground. I descend into the ground as well. It is cold, but not unpleasant. I am going deeper and deeper into the death.

It is collecting and gathering together – like it is pooling in one place. It feels like the earth has become a womb and I am an embryo. The blood has become an embryo. I am enjoying being there. It is peaceful and safe. There is a kind of gentle flowing movement, and I am part of that movement. There is just a beautiful peace about it all. I am very tiny. I look up and there seems to be something like a vortex which is soft and caressing. It touches me on the head. No one is anywhere near, yet I don't feel alone. It feels like a higher power is with me. This experience is so incredible – like I am cradled in the womb of the earth with a Godlike energy all around me.

A high percentage of clients who work with music and imagery have spiritual experiences. Many of them are agnostics and are, therefore, quite surprised to have a *real* spiritual experience. By *real* spiritual experience, I mean an experience that comes from deep inside you, as opposed to going to church and being told about spiritual matters. Many people go to church and believe intellectually in a higher power, but that does not automatically mean that they have actually experienced the higher power.

Energized Power

While energized power can be related to physical power, it is more than physical energy. Energized power can come from intense feelings, such as anger, passion, or joy. If you have experienced intense anger towards someone and found yourself cleaning the house vigorously with this anger energy, then you have experienced a form of energized power.

A powerful person in my life once told me that I could not succeed at a certain project I was working on. This pronouncement made me very angry. However, instead of giving up, I transformed my anger into energy that I poured into my project, which subsequently became a tremendous success. I attribute part of this success to my having transformed the anger energy into energized energy. If anger gets stuck, however, it becomes stagnant and is not only useless, but can be harmful to our mental and physical health. Energized anger, on the other hand, is more like a mountain stream that flows with tremendous energy, cleansing everything in its path and creating a refreshing energy that people are drawn towards.

Another example of energized power is when you feel very intensely about a subject or cause. For example, I know someone who loves animals with a passion and used her passionate energy to start an organization that takes pets to nursing homes, psychiatric hospitals, etc., for a therapeutic use. Turning your passion into a business or something positive can be extremely rewarding and is an excellent way to get in touch with energized power.

Physical Power

No one is anywhere near, yet I don't feel alone. It feels like a higher power is with me. This experience is so incredible – like I am cradled in the womb of the earth with a God-like energy all around me.

Not everyone is blessed with a strong athletic body. Some people are born to do cartwheels, it seems, while others of us are born to watch with wonder and sometimes envy. A certain sense of power comes from sheer physical achievement. For example, long-distance runners report a high or altered state after running a long distance. Similarly, many great athletes have described going into altered states while playing their sport.

But you don't have to be a great athlete to experience feelings of power from physical activity. One time while cross-country skiing in a park with large rolling hills, I found myself soaring down a medium-sized hill, unmarred by ski, animal or human tracks. I felt as if immersed in a sea of white – as if being one with the snow. For a few moments I felt as if I were in an altered state with no sense of time or place – just a vastness where only white and purity could exist. This is the kind of power that can come from a physical experience.

Many other examples may be given. For example, you may sense it on a long walk, while swimming, dancing or engaging in any other kind of physical activity. Being very athletic or strong is not necessarily a requirement, but it is possible that very athletic people feel this kind of power more often than the rest of us.

If you have not experienced physical power, you will have an opportunity later in this chapter to experience it in your mind with the help of music. This exercise is particularly helpful for people who have always wanted to dance or perform some other physical activity that they have never been able to do, as it can increase their sense of power. It can also be a wonderful experience for people with disabilities who cannot attain this kind of power any other way.

Power from Risk Taking

Some people thrive on risk taking, while others find risk taking extremely stressful. By *risk taking* I mean such things as skydiving, bunge jumping, taking big financial risks, starting your own business, etc. However, defining risk is difficult, since the concept is perceived differently by different people. Taking a risk is a way of stretching ourselves outside of our comfort zone in order to achieve personal growth. For example, if you suffer from a phobia of elevators, taking a risk could be just walking by elevators.

Getting on a plane for the first time was a tremendous risk to one of my clients who suffered a severe plane phobia. I'm sure you will be able instantly to come up with your own list of personal risk-taking activities. If you have fantasized about dangerous risk-taking activities like sky-diving, etc., the safest way to approximate this feeling is internally through your imagination. Take a moment to search your mind for examples of what you consider a risk. Put them into three categories:

1. Risks that are scary but possibly achievable in my lifetime:

_____

_____

_____

_____

_____

_____

2. Risks that could help me grow as a person:

_____

_____

_____

_____

_____

_____

3. Risks that I find fascinating, but consider impossible for me to tackle:

_____

_____

_____

_____

_____

_____

Power from Love

Love is a force that is very difficult to describe as witnessed by countless attempts over the ages. Some people say it is an energy; some people say love is giving to others unconditionally. The chorus of a John Denver song, *Perhaps Love,* expresses the difficulty of describing love and emphasizes that it is a matter of perception:[1]

Perhaps Love

Perhaps love to some is like a cloud
To some as strong as steel.
For some a way of living,
For some a way to feel.
And some say love is holding on
And some say letting go.
And some say love is everything,
Some say they don't know.
Perhaps love is like the ocean,
Full of conflict – full of pain.
Like a fire when it's cold outside,
Thunder when it rains.
If I should live forever
And all my dreams come true,
My memories of love will be of you.

This powerful force is something that we can get in touch with by just thinking of a past experience. Thinking of love as a kind of power is important. Love cannot be forced. An example is a woman named Irelandi who was having relationship and self-esteem problems. None of her relationships seemed to work out personally or professionally, including the one with her boss, who fired her. As a result, she was deep in the throes of depression and the only thing in life that really brought her relief was the love for her cats. One day she ran across a book that said, if you are having trouble with love and relationships, just love whatever you can. This gave her permission to just love her cats and feel OK about it, instead of being critical of herself for not feeling love for any person. If you are at a time in your life where you can only love your collection of salt and pepper shakers, just love it with a passion, and that love will grow into the ability to love in other areas.

To help explore the love force inside of you, refer to the exercise portion of this chapter. The music will help you experience this force in a way that is appropriate for you.

Power over Food

All of us struggle with power issues at various times. For example, a common issue is the power that food has over people. When you are overweight and rationally know that eating the wrong foods may shorten your life or increase your chance of having a stroke, your unconscious can take over with the result that food suddenly takes on tremendous power. For example, at luncheons I often hear women talk about being overweight, yet no one turns down dessert. It is almost as if they reason that this has been served to me, so I must eat it.

Occasionally, however, I meet a diabetic who has the power to say no to dessert, or a person who has developed strong convictions about what he or she wants to eat. The bottom line is that a small, apparently powerless dish of ice cream or a bag of greasy potato chips can wield gargantuan power over us. *Think of the absurdity of this.*

Through guided imagery and music you can take your power back. The power must come through inner sources. Your head can talk to you all day about what is good, but if inwardly you feel powerless, the bad food choices will win out.

A woman named Tracy, in one of my classes, was about 40 pounds overweight when she started the class. After completing the exercise at the end of this chapter on Power over Food, she had a big smile on her face. She said that she had visualized one giant pea left on her plate and there was this tremendous struggle about whether or not to eat it.

> *She had visualized one giant pea left on her plate and there was this tremendous struggle about whether or not to eat it.*

My old childhood message which was literally branded in me was 'clean up your plate or else you will be punished!' versus my new self that said, 'I am full, stop eating.' The music brought up imagery of struggling with these two voices and the giant pea had tremendous power over me. This struggle seemed like it lasted for a long time until finally the music helped me feel a sense of power over the situation. All of a sudden that one pea hopped off the plate and landed in the compost pile and subsequently produced many more peas. This made me feel like it was OK to not eat every bite on my plate. Happily, I was able to overcome the giant pea and peacefully make the choice not to eat the last bit just because it was left on my plate.

The experience was really amazing and now I feel a new sense of inner power. I have struggled with this so long. It is as if I have to eat every bite on my plate or I feel tremendous guilt. I know it sounds crazy, but that was the childhood message that keeps affecting me daily and keeps my weight a constant battle. Now, as a result of this experience with the music, I feel an inner shift has occurred.

If food has power over you, try the music exercises in this chapter to help you bolster your inner power resources. Write your feelings in the space provided after each exercise.

Exercises: Inner Power

Quiet Inner Power Exercise

> Musical choices: Janalea Hoffman's *Musical Acupuncture,*
> Samuel Barber's *Adagio for Strings,* Haydn's *Cello Concerto,*
> *2nd movement,* or Beethoven's *6th Symphony* – also known
> as the *Pastoral Symphony.*

To get in touch with your quiet inner power, have your music selection ready to be turned on, read through this script in a meditative mode, then sit or lie down in a relaxed position and surrender yourself to the music and the moment.

When the music begins, just listen and contemplate the idea of quiet inner power. The music may remind you of a quiet place in nature, either a place you have been or perhaps a place you have never seen. Be open to letting the music and your subconscious take you to the spot where you can best experience quiet inner power. The place will speak to you of inner quiet. It may be a quiet lake gently lapping on the shore. Despite the gentle energy, there is a constancy to the rhythm and a power that reaches you at a deep feeling level. Or it may be the quiet power of a forest, in which each tree exudes its own special energy. You might want to stand or lie down on the forest floor and soak up all of this quiet inner power. The trees are anxious to share their energy and will not judge you. Be open to their help in your quest for quiet inner power.

To achieve inner power, you may spend the entire time in one spot, or you may need to gain power from several locations. Relax now and enjoy your journey. After the music ends, record your experiences by writing down any imagery you experienced, as well as emotional and physical sensations:

_____

_____

_____

_____

_____

Spiritual Power Exercise

> Musical choices: Janalea Hoffman's *Musical Hypnosis*, Rachmaninoff's *Vespers*, Palestrina's, *Missa Marcella papae*, or Alan Hohvaness's *Mysterious Mountain*.

When the music starts, relax and prepare yourself for leaving your earthly self to explore your spiritual side. This might mean feeling extremely sensitive to your surroundings, seeing, hearing or sensing angels or spiritual guides. Be open to whatever form they may appear in. Perhaps you are about to experience a form of spiritual guide that you were unable to imagine before today. Tell yourself that you commit to opening yourself to only the highest vibrations and their messages.

Also tell yourself that you want information about any barriers you might unknowingly have put up to shut out spiritual guidance. Perhaps it was too scary in the past. Perhaps you wanted to be in control and felt that if you listened too closely to guidance, you might be told to do things you wouldn't like. Give up control now!

Have faith that your guides know your highest good much better than you do and that they will guide you to greater joy. See yourself shedding layers of fear about your spirituality like a snake sheds its skin. As the fear peels off, feel yourself reach a deep place of silence where the voice of guidance can be heard and followed.

After the music ends, record your experiences and emotions:

_____

_____

_____

_____

_____

_____

_____

_____

_____

_____

Energized Power Exercise

Musical choices: Aaron Copland's *Appalachian Spring and Rodeo,* Rachmaninoff's *3rd Symphony,* or Mahler's *8th Symphony.*

When the music begins, you will be reminded of something you have wanted to accomplish for a long time – something you may have tried but failed at, or something you have yet to try. Or the music may remind you of something you have never thought about achieving. Suddenly the music gives you the courage to try something that previously seemed very difficult or even impossible.

Even though you have selected something very difficult, know that you will succeed. The power of the music will combine with your inner resources to give you the strength to accomplish whatever you want to. Granted, there may be periods of struggle or resistance, but allow yourself to observe your experiences. Trust that the struggle or resistance will end and that you will experience a strong sense of having overcome something. Trust the music to guide you through the resistance or struggle and take you to the triumphant feeling.

After the music has ended, record your experiences and emotions:

_____

_____

_____

_____

_____

_____

_____

_____

_____

Physical Power Exercise

Musical choices: Richard Strauss's *Till Eulenspiegel*, Georges Bizet's *Carmen* or *Symphony in C* , Bach's *Brandenberg Concertos 1 through 6*, Nikolai Rimsky-Korsakov's *Scheherazade*, or *Russian Easter Overture*.

When the music starts, begin imagining yourself as the conductor. After being timid at first, perhaps, you may realize that being a conductor can be a very physical, almost athletic experience. Feel the music in your body. The rhythm is strong and you experience it at a cellular level. You must convey this feeling to the players. Give yourself permission to use your whole body to conduct the orchestra. Think of Whoopi Goldberg in *Sister Act*, the movie where she throws her whole body into conducting the gospel choir. This may not be your style, but allow your whole being to get into the music, nevertheless. Feel a commitment to communicate these rhythms to the players you are conducting. Gradually, you'll feel yourself completely lost in the conducting, your arms becoming one with the baton and the players. The activity almost turns into a dance.

After you have finished conducting the orchestra, you may want to dance, or do gymnastics or some other physical activity to the music. Allow the music to guide you. Now let yourself imagine tackling physical feats that you never before dreamed possible. Experience how great it feels to have physical power. For example, exhilarate at being able to ice skate and do a double axle effortlessly. If you start to doubt your ability to visualize yourself having physical power, be aware of your resistance to the process. If you have the ability to visualize an ice cream cone, you also have the ability to visualize yourself achieving extraordinary physical feats. If you find yourself struggling, be aware and observe the process. You don't have to worry about what you will visualize because your body and subconscious will know which physical feats are important for you to achieve. Relax and enjoy the music and your new sense of physical power.

After the music has ended, record your experiences and emotions:

Power Through Risk Taking Exercise

Musical choices: Richard Strauss's *Death and Transfiguration,* Beethoven's *Appasionata for Piano* or *1st Symphony.*

When the music starts, let your mind search for all the activities that you would classify as risk taking. Think of them as scrolling by on a computer screen. As they move by, you may visualize some of them more graphically. The music will guide you, and at some point you will decide to picture yourself going through the actions of deciding to take the risk and then visualizing it step by step in your mind. Part of this process will be experiencing some anxiety before you start, possibly some resistance, but then going ahead and following through with the actions. Notice the sensations you experience as you complete your risk-taking goal. How does it feel? Was it scary? Do you want to repeat it in your mind?

You may want to try other types of risks to see how they feel. Follow your feelings. If there is something you want to try, go ahead, knowing you have the power in your imagination to take the risk. Let the power of the music give you strength. If your rational mind is critical about this exercise, gently shut it off in the knowledge that anything you think or feel is valid. Shutting out critical thoughts can be accomplished in many ways. One way is to visualize a screen coming down over the critical area of your brain and blocking it off. If you really want to discipline your thoughts, creative answers will emerge. The music really helps in this process. You have the power to cut off the criticisms and the "I can'ts." Enjoy your journey!

After the music has ended, record your experiences and emotions:

Power from Love Exercise

> Musical choices: Janalea Hoffman's *Musical Massage*, Rachmaninoff's *2nd piano Concerto, 2nd movement*, Rachmaninoff's *Love Theme* (18th Variation - from *Rhapsody on a Theme of Paganini*), Ralph Vaughan Williams' *A Lark Ascending*, and Claude Debussy's, *Prelude to the Afternoon of a Faun*.

Our conception of movement is connected to something that occurs in our real world. Movement is usually thought of as physical movement. Yet, there can be a movement of the mind and the spirit too. Indeed, we often say that we have been *moved* by an event or by something that someone said. In this way we are moved in much the same sense that an object is moved from the shade into the sun. The object has not physically moved, but it is different now because it is in the sun instead of in the shade. This is similar to how love moves us into new territory within ourselves. Many things can move us, and one of the most powerful of these is love. Love can bring our spirit from the darkest of shadows into the brightest of sunlight.

As the music begins, let love begin to take you on a journey. Let it change what you think about, what you feel, and let it also change you in those many subtle ways that are so difficult to describe. Don't try to control or direct these changes. Just let them occur as you experience the love force. Flow with the love like a tide that you trust completely. And as you receive this love, you may want to return it to other people in your life who could benefit from this energy. (If you are doing this with a group, you might think of the love coming from each individual into you and you passing it on.)

Sense the power that unites you with yourself like an umbilical cord unites the child with its mother. Feel yourself blending together with people in your life and thereby becoming a part of the others. The more you blend into a single harmony, the more likely you are to find that light of ultimate peace, of ultimate harmony. And if you find this light, you will probably also find it difficult to feel apart from the others any longer, for you will feel a buoyancy that will transcend your own consciousness and travel through the group in currents of joyous caring. And in this harmony, this peace in oneness, you will sense the beat of everyone's heart as the beat of your own heart.

Record your experiences in the spaces below. Be sure to express everything you felt even if it seems insignificant. It is important to write it down:

Power over Food Exercise

> Musical choices: *Beethoven's 9th - 3rd and 4th movements.*
> Janalea Hoffman's *Musical Massage* , Faure's *Requiem*,
> Johannes Brahms' *A German Requiem*, or Richard Strauss's
> *Death and Transfiguration.*

As the music begins, relax as much as possible and listen to the music. Tell your muscles that they might as well give up their control because you are serious about relaxing to the music, blocking all other issues out of your mind in preference for this meditative experience. You begin to relax, which feels really good. Then you notice the conflict in the music. The music becomes your teacher about conflict. You feel the pull of silly things like cupcakes having power over you, and the other more powerful side of you demands to win out. Fully experience the struggle of giving over your power to food. Fully experience the absurdity of allowing a little piece of pie that you could step on and destroy in one second having power over a grown person like you. See the absurdity of choosing bad food over good health. The music will take you through this struggle.

Then in the midst of the struggle, your subconscious will bring up the memory of being in your mother's womb. Everything was peaceful and quiet. You had power. Your every need was fulfilled. You had plenty of nourishment and you felt secure and cradled by the sides of your mother's uterus. Life was safe and secure. Feel the power you felt at having all your needs met.

Let the music guide you into a gradual build-up of inner power. You feel your sense of power growing from a deep place inside. Any resistance is being healed and repaired from inside, as the music takes you out of the conflict into a place of beauty and triumphant overcoming. The overcoming is so joyful that you want to dance and express it both physically as well as internally. For example, you see yourself going to a party boasting an abundant buffet where you make healthy food choices, rejecting fattening, sweet and other unhealthy foods and beverages. You feel so proud to have strong convictions about what you put into your body. You feel strongly that *this is your body temple and that it must not be violated.* The feelings of overcoming become stronger and stronger, and as the music swells so does your inner sense of power and self-esteem. The agony of utter helplessness is gone, crushed by this new sense of power, sensitivity and confidence.

Use the space below to record your experiences, including your imagery, feelings, sensations, etc.:

Comments on Selected Music from Inner Power Exercises

When an artist/composer works through their emotional issues in a piece of music, this energy comes through and can be very helpful in a therapeutic situation. For example, when you see a painting that obviously has "struggle" as a theme, it automatically taps into your psyche and helps you relate to your own struggle issues. The same is true with music. Listening to Beethoven's music written when he was working through a severe emotional crisis helps draw out that energy inside of you. If you aren't having an emotional crisis, you would probably experience the triumphant or overcoming aspect of the music and not concentrate as much on the struggle aspects.

The following comments on some of the specific music pieces may give you some ideas of how you can use this music in a therapeutic way. The observations are based on my personal inner work using the music and also using it with clients. You may experience something completely different, although most of these comments were universally felt by the other participants.

Quiet Inner Power

A *Lark Ascending* by Ralph Vaughn Williams

In this piece there is a lightness – a sense of quiet flight. It does sound like its title. The lyrical line makes you visualize gentle birds joyfully ascending in the sky. There is a sense of peace – like it is a sunny day with no threat of conflict or storm – just total peace on a day devoted to something lighthearted like kite flying.

Mysterious Mountain by Alan Hovhaness

Hovhaness remarked about his music, "I've always listened to my own voice. I was discontented with the kind of music that everyone said that I should write – all clever and dissonant, intellectualized. I wanted to write music that was deeply felt, music that would move people." I find that Hovhaness' music takes us to spiritual heights and to inner places that you may not have previously explored. He was very interested in metaphysical and spiritual matters. This energy comes through in his music.

6th Symphony by Beethoven also known as *The Pastoral Symphony.*

This was written to evoke a pastoral scene, influenced by Beethoven's surroundings. You can hear the influence of the alberti bass – arpeggios which sound like a clippity cloppity of horse hooves. This symphony was influenced by the beautiful pastures in Beethoven's area. The music paints a beautiful picture of this kind of quiet nature scene. Beethoven's music in general is a good example of struggle – resolution. He uses conflict in the music and resolves it quickly, however, this symphony fits well with quiet inner power because it is one of Beethoven's more serene musical compositions.

Spiritual Power

Vespers by Rachmaninoff

This is a chorale work that transports you to spiritual heights. It will elicit imagery about your own inner journey that is unique for you. If you are feeling out of touch with your spiritual life, try this music with the spiritual power exercise. You will become a believer in the power of music to transport you from one level of consciousness to another in a very short time.

Energized Power

Carmen Suite by Georges Bizet

There is a feeling of rhythmic flow throughout this piece, even in the quiet places. It is as though the rhythm takes your hand and keeps leading you towards your goal. Therefore, it is very energizing for the listener. It is good for passivity problems. If you feel stuck, it can help mobilize your energy to take appropriate action.

Appalachian Spring by Aaron Copland

This piece starts out quiet, but with a sense that something is going to happen – as if the quiet music is a premonition of a more dramatic event to come. Humor, drama, optimism and melancholy are all expressed at different times in this music. Great for inner imagery and inner power work.

Physical Power

Fanfare for the Common Man by Aaron Copland

Fanfare for the Common Man is a dramatic and powerful example of music that elicits strong imagery in the listener. It is great for increasing inner power. You may experience resistance to it if you are inclined to resist your own power. Be aware of this when you listen, and allow the powerful energy to help you tap into your own inner resources. If you find yourself having a negative reaction to it, be a careful observer of your imagery and feelings. If you stay with the imagery, you will learn more about yourself and what is going on internally.

Till Eulenspiegel by Richard Strauss

Till Eulenspiegel is a comic piece based on the antics of a north German rapscallion, who gets into all kinds of mischief as you will hear in the music. The great youthful energy and humor in this piece are why it can work well for eliciting physical power.

Power from Risk Taking

Beethoven's *Piano Sonata No. 23 in F Minor, Op. 57*, also referred to as the "*Appassionata*" *Sonata*

As its name implies, this piece is passionate with dramatic highs and lows. Beethoven began work on this sonata in 1804 when he was 33 years old. It was completed a year later. During this time he passed through a severe emotional crisis because he knew his deafness would be complete soon. This meant giving up his career as a performer and never hearing his greatest works. This is a tremendously powerful piece of music and can be extremely helpful in drawing out passion and energy in the listener.

Violin Concerto by Alban Berg

Berg was known for his dissonant compositions. There are some melodious passages, but for the most part this music brings up frustration, struggle and sometimes anger. This is good music to use if you want to explore suppressed anger. Use it sparingly, and have more consonant music ready to conclude your session so you end with an uplifting feeling of having overcome the conflict.

Death and Transfiguration by Richard Strauss

This music is about a man on his deathbed. He is fondly remembering childhood and his youthful prowess in an effort to escape from his pain. You hear the struggle in the music. His only comfort comes from a faith in an afterlife. When his body finally succumbs to death, the music crescendos into a glorious soulful melody that transports you to an ethereal place. The music ends with a feeling of deep serenity. This is wonderful music to explore any inner struggles you may have. This music helps you overcome obstacles. Use it for giving yourself energy for positive changes.

Power over Food

Isle of the Dead by Rachmaninoff

This powerful tone poem can take you to subconscious places that need to be transformed. The music was inspired when Rachmaninoff saw a painting with the same title. It depicts an island that is mostly cliffs rising out of the ocean with a tiny opening through the jagged rock with a boat moving through with a white coffin balancing tentatively with the rocking waves. The painting as well as the music were meant to create a feeling rather than tell a story. The music brings up thick foggy images that may need letting go – perhaps old parts of your psyche that need to die and be reborn so you can grow.

Requiem by Brahm's

Brahms wrote his *Requiem* as a direct result of emotional pain caused by his friend's death, the great composer Robert Schumann. He started the *Requiem* but didn't complete it until after his mother's death. He poured his grief struggle into this musical masterpiece. There is an emotional intensity to the music as well as a transcendent quality. It leaves you with a feeling of spiritual overcoming. This magnificent music can help with overcoming any situation. Use this when you need help moving out of a stuck place.

References

Music and Your Heart
1 Cushman, A. "Drumming to the Rhythms of Life." *Yoga Journal*. Jan. - Feb., 1993.
2 Brown, B.B. *Supermind*. 1980, New York, Harper and Row.
3 Darner, C.L. "Sound Pulses and the Heart." *The Journal of the Acoustical Society of America*, 1966, pp. 414-416, and Brady, J.P., Luborsky, L., and Kron, R. *Behavior Therapy*, 1974, pp 203-209.
4 *Deep Daydreams*. Composed and produced by Janalea Hoffman, 1986.
5 *Musical Hypnosis*. Composed and produced by Janalea Hoffman, 1993.
6 *Therapeutic Drumming*. Composed and produced by Janalea Hoffman, 1993.
7 Leonard, G. *The Silent Pulse*. E.P. Dutton, New York, 1978.
8 Leonard, G. *The Silent Pulse*. E.P. Dutton, New York, 1978.
9 Diamond, M.D., John. *The Life Energy of Music, Vol. 1*. Archaeus Press, Valley Cottage, New York, 1983.
10 Ostrander, S., and Schroeder, L. *Superlearning 2000*. Delacorte Press, New York, 1994.
11 Ostrander, S., and Schroeder, L. *Superlearning 2000*. Delacorte Press, New York, 1994.
12 Pollack, C. "Suggestology and Suggestopedia Revisited." *Journal of Suggestive-Accelerative Learning and Teaching*, 1979, Vol. 4, pp 16-31.
13 Brown, B.B. *New Mind, New Body*. Anchor Press / Doubleday, New York, 1977.
14 Ostrander, S., and Schroeder, L. *Superlearning 2000*. Delacorte Press, New York, 1994.
15 Blanchard, B.E. "The Effect of Music on Pulse Rate, Blood Pressure, and Final Exam Scores of University Students." *The Journal of Sports Medicine*, 1979, Vol. 19, pp 305-307.
16 *Mind, Body, Tempo*. Composed by Janalea Hoffman, produced by Unity Village, Unity Village, MO, 1986.
17 Hoffman, J., Summers, S., Neff, J., Hanson, S., Pierce, J. "The Effects of 60-Beats-Per-Minute Music on Test Taking Anxiety Among Nursing Students." *Journal of Nursing Education*, February, 1980.

Musical Biofeedback
1 *Musical Biofeedback*. Composed and Produced by Janalea Hoffman, 1993.
2 Pelletier, K.C. *Mind as Healer, Mind as Slayer, A Holistic Approach to Preventing Stress Disorders*. Delecorte Press / Seymour Lawrence, San Francisco, CA, 1977.

3   Green, E. and Green, A. *Beyond Biofeedback*. Delacorte Press / Seymour Lawrence, San Francisco, CA, 1977.
4   Meyer, J.S., Saka, F., Yamaguchi, F., Yamamoto, M., and Shaw, T. "Regional Changes in Cerebral Blood Flow During Standard Behavioral Activation in Patients with Disorders of Speech and Mentation Compared to Normal Volunteers." *Brain and Language*, Jan., 1980, Vol. 9, pp 61-77.
5   Lang, P., Kozak, M. J., Miller, G.A., Levin, D., and McLean, A. "Emotional Imagery: Conceptual Structure of Pattern of Somato-Visceral Response." *Psychophysiology*, 1980, Vol. 17, pp 179-192.
6   Schwartz, G., Brown, S., Lynn, A., and Geoffrey, L. "Facial Muscle Patterning and Subjective Experience During Affective Imagery: Sex Differences." *Psychophysiology,* Jan., 1980, Vol. 17, pp 75-82.
7   Frostig, M., and Maslow, P. "Neuropsychological Contributions to Education." *Journal of Learning Disabilities*, 1979, Vol. 12, pp 538-552.

Music and Lowering Blood Pressure

1   Kaplan, M.D., Norman, William, and Wilkins. *Clinical Hypertension*. Baltimore, MD, 6th Ed., 1994.
2   Guyton, A.C. *Textbook of Medical Physiology*. Saunders, Philadelphia, 1971.
3   Boyd, W. *An Introduction to the Study of Disease*. Lea and Febiger, Philadelphia, 1962.
4   Harrison. *Principles of Internal Medicine*. McGraw Hill, New York, 1991.
5   Selye, H. "Confusion and Controversy in the Stress Field." *Journal of Human Stress*, 1975, Vol. 1, pp 37-44.
6   Selye, H. "Confusion and Controversy in the Stress Field." *Journal of Human Stress*, 1975, Vol. 1, pp 37-44.
7   Richter-Heinrich, E. "Psychophysiological Personality Patterns of Hypertensive and Normotensive Subjects." *Psychotherapy and Psychomatics*, 1970, pp 332-340.
8   Schacter, J. "Pain, Fear and Anger in Hypertensives and Normotensives. A Psychophysiological Study." *Psychosomatic Medicine*, 1957, pp 152-162.
9   Shapiro, A.P. "An Experimental Study of Comparative Responses of Blood Pressure to Different Noxious Stimuli." *Journal of Chronic Disease*, 1961, Vol. 13, pp 293-311.
10 Agras, S., Taylor, C.B., Kraemer, H.C., Allen, R.A., and Schneider, J.A. "Relaxation Training – Twenty-Four Hour Blood Pressure Reductions." *Archives of General Psychiatry*, 1980, Vol. 37, pp 859-863.
11 Jacobson, E. *Progressive Relaxation*. University of Chicago Press, Chicago, 1962.
12 Wilhelmsen, L. and Stresser, T. on behalf of the Study Collaborators WHO-WHL Hypertension Management Audit Project, *Journal of Human Hypertension*, 1993, Vol. 7, pp 257-263.

13 Caldwell, J.R., Cobb, S., Dowling, M.D., and others. "The Drop-out Problem in Anti-Hypertensive Treatment: A Pilot Study of Social and Emotional Factors Influencing a Patient's Ability to Follow Antihypertensive Treatment." *Journal of Chronic Disease*, 1970, Vol. 22, p 579.

14 Finnerty, F.A., Jr., Mattie, E.C., and Finnerty, F.A., III. "Hypertension in the Inner City: 1. Analysis of Clinic Dropouts." *Circulation*, 1973, Vol. 47, p 73.

15 Fletcher, S.W., Appel, F. A., and Bourgois, M. "Improving Emergency-room Patient Follow-up in a Metropolitan Teaching Hospital: Effect of a Follow-up Clerk." *New England Journal of Medicine*, 1974, Vol. 291, p 385.

16 Finnerty, F. A., Jr., Mattie, E.C., and Finnerty, F.A., III. "Hypertension in the Inner City: 1. Analysis of Clinic Dropouts." *Circulation*, 1973, Vol. 47, p 73.

17 Sackett, D.L. "The Hypertensive Patient: 5. Compliance with Therapy." *Canadian Medical Association Journal*, 1979, Vol. 121, pp 259-261.

18 Sackett, D. L., Haynes, R.B., Gibson, E.S., and others. "Randomized Clinical Trail of Strategies for Improving Medication Compliance in Primary Hypertension." *Lancet*, 1975, Vol. 1, p 1205.

19 Haynes, R.B., Sackett, D.L., Gibson, E.S., and others. "Improvement of Medication Compliance in Uncontrolled Hypertension." *Lancet*, 1976, Vol. 1, p 1265.

20 Sackett, D. L., Haynes, R.B., Gibson, E.S., and others. "Randomized Clinical Trail of Strategies for Improving Medication Compliance in Primary Hypertension." *Lancet*, 1975, Vol. 1, p 1205.

Using Music to Help Contact the Inner Child

1 *When You Wish Upon A Star*. Performed by Daniel Kobialka, arranger, producer, Andy Kulberg, Li-sem Enterprises, Inc., 1988.

Music and Codependency

1 *Only You*. From *Rock Around the Clock*. Words and music by Buck Ram and Ande Rand, 1955.

2 *Upside Down*. Words and music by Bernie Edwards and Nile Rodgers, performed by Diana Ross, 1980.

3 *How Am I Supposed To Live Without You*. Words and music by Michael Bolton and Doug James, performed by Michael Bolton, 1990.

4 *Achy Breaky Heart*. Words and music by Don Von Tress, performed by Billy Ray Cyrus, 1991.

5 *Lonely Ol' Night*. John Mellencamp, 1986.

6 *I Want To Be Happy.* From *No, No, Nanette.* Words by Irving Caesar, music by Vincent Youmans, 1924.

7 *I Have a Tendency for Codependency.* Words and music by Terri Sharp and Michael Brown, performed by Greg Tamblyn, 1992.

Positive Songs

1 *On A Clear Day You Can See Forever.* Words by Alan Jay Lerner, music by Burton Lane, 1966.

2 *The Way He Makes Me Feel.* From the original motion picture sound-track, Barbra Streisand's, *Yentl,* 1983.

3 *It's In Every One of Us.* Performed and written by David Pomeranz, 1975.

4 *Gonna Build a Mountain.* From *Stop the World - I Want to Get Off.* Words and music by Leslie Bricusse and Anthony Newley, 1962.

5 *Climb Every Mountain.* From *The Sound of Music* Words by Richard Rogers and words by Oscar Hammerstein, 1959.

6 Diamond, M.D., J. *The Life Energy of Music, Vol. 1.* Archaeus Press, Valley Cottage, New York, 1983.

7 *Unconditional Love (The Story of Evy).* Words, music, and performed by Greg Tamblyn, 1993.

8 *You Can't Blame the Wreck On the Train.* Words and music by Terri Sharp, performed by Greg Tamblyn, 1992.

9 *Let Me Remember.* Words by Shanti, music by Oman Ken, performed by Cathy Robel, 1982.

10 *Gotta Find A Better Way.* Words, music, and performed by Ken Medema, 1993.

11 *Music of the Night.* From *Phantom of the Opera.* Words by Charles Hart, music by Andrew Lloyd Webber, 1987.

Inner Power through Music

1 *Perhaps Love.* Words and music by John Denver, 1980.

Sources of Sounds

Therapeutic music by Janalea Hoffman

Musical Acupuncture. An innovative concept in music therapy developed by Janalea Hoffman. Experience how music can conduct and move energy in your body very similar to an acupuncture treatment - without needles! Particularly effective for chronic pain such as arthritis, back pain, headaches, etc. Specially metered music at 50 beats per minute.

Musical Massage. Written and performed with the idea of healing and nurturing. Instead of just listening with your ears, Hoffman suggests that you think of your entire body feeling the vibration of the beautiful music as though it was a musical massage.

Musical Biofeedback. Designed to help empower individuals to control their body rhythms. Specially metered musical rhythms are used as a learning technique instead of biofeedback equipment to help you learn how to tune into your body, so that you can lower your heart rate, blood pressure, and breathing rate. Music starts at exactly 80 beats a minute and gradually slows to 50 beats a minute.

Musical Hypnosis. Specially composed metered music designed to take you from a stressed heart rate of 80 beats a minute down to a relaxed heart rate of 50 beats a minute. You can use this tape to simply slow yourself down physiologically or you can use it to facilitate a state of hypnosis.

Deep Daydreams. Hoffman, inspired by nature's own soothing sounds of water in a gentle brook, wrote this metered music to lower heart rate and blood pressure. One side exactly 50 beats a minute, one side exactly 60 beats a minute. Also, an excellent tool for accelerated learning.

The Dolphin Song - A Children's Meditation Tape. Relaxation games and guided imagery with specially composed music teaches your child relaxation and concentration techniques. For example, kids learn about their own body rhythms in an imaginative game with Frankie the Flute. Recommended ages are 2 to 11.

Therapeutic Drumming. Gentle feminine drumming done in beats of three to correspond to a normal heart beat. Ideal for Shamanic work to help you into a hypnotic state as your body tries to synchronize with the drum.

Music for Mellow Minds. Clear out your stock of over the counter sleeping aids and put this tape on. Hoffman's specially composed piano music metered at 60 beats a minute produces a soothing and relaxing experience. Side 2 is composed specifically as a guided music meditation for sleep and tension control.

Mind Body Tempo. The rhythms in this tape produce a synthesis of mind and body. Side one highlights piano music at 60 beats a minute with orchestration of flute, violins, cello, and clarinet. Hoffman has created a soothing piano selection on Side 2 with a mixture of east and west with harp, flute, and piano.

Music to Facilitate Imagery. Anything you desire - from prosperity to a thinner body - must be created in your mind first. This tape will help you develop your ability to visualize and therefore create your own reality.

Crisis Tape. A crisis is like a baby's cry - it usually comes at inconvenient times - often in the middle of the night. *The Crisis Tape* comforts and reassures, as an adjunct to therapy and in those times when outside help is not available.

Music, Imagery, and Parkinson's. A very specialized experience for people who have Parkinson's Disease, their caregivers, and loved ones. Look beyond drugs to help manage Parkinson's. Exercises with specially metered music using techniques for tremor management and other non-pharmaceutical approaches.

Touched By the Light. With Hoffman's music in the background, this gently guided visualization by a nurse, hospice chaplain, provides the listener with a glimpse of what may lie beyond life as we know it. Experiencing a peaceful view of the dying process can bring a greater sense of hope and acceptance. Designed for the patient and their loved ones.

Videos by Janalea Hoffman

Rhythmic Medicine. A beautiful nature relaxation video with specially metered music synchronized with the visuals. See the snow fall at exactly 60 beats a minute and experience the flow of water at 50 beats a minute. An open-eyed way to practice musical biofeedback.

Rhythmic Medicine - Instructional Video. Learn how to use music as a teaching tool directly from Janalea Hoffman. Excellent for health care professionals who know there is power in music, but do not know how to apply it to their work.

Music by Greg Tamblyn

The Shootout at the I'm OK, You're OK Corral. In order to heal, we must be able to laugh at ourselves and recognize our dysfunction! If you are, or have been in a 12-step program and understand codependency, this tape is a must for your music library.

Greg Tamblyn, N.C.W.* (No Credentials Whatsoever*). A follow-up to the first album. More powerful songs about codependency.

Music by Ken Medema

Where Do I Go From Here? A Musical Dialogue in the Journey of Loss and Grief. This series of tapes contains over three hours of listening. The special blend of music and conversation "marries" our "head knowledge" with our "heart feelings" about loss and grief and will give each listener a healthy and constructive vehicle for dealing with this profound and often unspoken human experience.

Music by Daniel Kobialka

When You Wish Upon a Star. A beautiful, fully orchestrated, all music version of some of our favorite children's lullabies, arranged by Kobialka to be played in a slow, soothing way that is almost certain to bring memories of childhood to mind.

Music by Gordon R. Hodas, M.D.

Stretch Yourself! Songs for Coping. A collection of 11 songs written for children and families. The songs can be used for individual, group, and family psychotherapy, etc. Songs promote wellness and examine developmental issues, as well as critical health threats such as adolescent suicide, child sexual abuse, and drug abuse. The major theme of these songs is that negative situations can be turned into positive. A user's guide booklet comes with the cassette.

ORDER FORM

Jamillan Press, Box 6431, Leawood, KS 66206

Mail my order to:

Name: _____

Address: _____

City: _____ State: _____ Zip: _____

Phone: _____ Check enclosed: _____

MC/Visa #: _____ Exp: _____

QTY		PRICE	TOTAL
By Janalea Hoffman:			
_____	**Book: *Rhythmic Medicine***	**$14.95**	_____
_____	Music cassette to accompany exercises in book, *Rhythmic Medicine*	$ 9.95	_____
_____	Rhythmic Medicine Relaxation Video	$49.95	_____
_____	Rhythmic Medicine Instructional Video	$34.95	_____
_____	Deep Daydreams Cassette **	$12.95	_____
_____	Deep Daydreams CD **	$16.95	_____
_____	Children's Meditation Tape Cassette	$ 9.95	_____
_____	Mind-Body Tempo Cassette **	$ 9.95	_____
_____	Music for Mellow Minds Cassette	$11.95	_____
_____	Music to Facilitate Imagery Cassette	$ 9.95	_____
_____	Music, Imagery, and Parkinsons Cassette	$11.95	_____
_____	Musical Acupuncture Cassette	$12.95	_____
_____	Musical Acupuncture CD (64 minutes)	$19.95	_____
_____	Musical Biofeedback Cassette	$12.95	_____
_____	Musical Hypnosis Cassette **	$12.95	_____
_____	Musical Massage Cassette **	$12.95	_____
_____	Musical Massage CD **	$14.95	_____
_____	Crisis Tape Cassette	$ 9.95	_____
_____	Touched By The Light Cassette	$ 9.95	_____
_____	Therapeutic Drumming Cassette **	$10.95	_____
By Greg Tamblyn:			
_____	The Shootout at the I'm OK, You're OK Corral	$10.95	_____
_____	Greg Tamblyn, N.C.W.	$10.95	_____
By Ken Medema:			
_____	Where Do I Go From Here? (3 Cassettes)	$29.95	_____
By Daniel Kobialka:			
_____	When You Wish Upon A Star **	$ 9.95	_____
By Gordon R. Hodas, M.D.:			
_____	Stretch Yourself! Songs for Coping w/Booklet	$14.95	_____

* Shipping _____

Total Enclosed _____

* **Shipping: Orders up to $50.00: add $2.50, from $50.00 - $100.00: add $3.50, over $100.00: add $5.00.**

** *These are all music tapes - no words are spoken on the tapes.*

*Please note: We honor your privacy.
your name is not provided to any other organization.*

THANK YOU